The
Complete

By Herbert S. FitzGibbon II
and Jeffrey N. Bairstow

Illustrated by Elmer Wexler

Racquet Sports Player

SIMON AND SCHUSTER
NEW YORK

Published by Simon and Schuster
A Division of Gulf & Western Corporation
Simon & Schuster Building
Rockefeller Center
1230 Avenue of the Americas
New York, New York 10020

Designed by Irving Perkins
Manufactured in the United States of America
1 2 3 4 5 6 7 8 9 10

Library of Congress Cataloging in Publication Data
FitzGibbon, Herbert S
The complete racquet sports player.

Bibliography: p.
1. Racket games. I. Bairstow, Jeffrey, date—
joint author. II. Title.
GV990.F57   796.34   79-22199
ISBN 0-671-24740-9

Contents

8   The Complete Racquet Sports Player

Foreword

Although I play all the major racquet sports—some at a high standard—play alone could not fully educate me in them. To acquire a greater understanding of these games in relation to each other, I had to observe and analyze them. I spent many hours watching and talking with experts in all the racquet sports discussed in this book. These people were lavish with their time and insights. Without them, the book could never have been completed.

Vic Niederhoffer took many hours out of his crowded business schedule to provide a wealth of background material on squash, racquetball and paddleball.

Vic Seixas, who has held national titles in tennis and squash, provided valuable insights into the relationships between these two games. Dave Benjamin, the director of racquet sports at Princeton University, also was most helpful here.

Clark Graebner and Sarah Danzig, who have won national championships in both tennis and platform tennis, commented freely on their sports.

John Halpern, squash entrepreneur and player, and Mel Sokolow, the national veterans doubles champion in squash, helped round out my knowledge of squash.

Margaret Varner Bloss is perhaps the most complete racquet sports player of them all, having held national titles in tennis, badminton and squash. Her experience in these three games was invaluable.

No man has thought more about racquetball than Charlie Brumfield. He and his coach, Carl Loveday, generously shared their great knowledge of this game and its relationship to the other racquet sports.

Badminton activists Rajiv Chandra, Paul de Loca, Hassan Dibb, Steve Edson and Chris Kinard gave freely of their time to complete my badminton education.

Steve Kraft (U.S. Tennis Association), Chuck Leve (U.S. Racquetball Association, Gloria Dillenbeck (American Platform Tennis Association) and Darwin Kingsley (U.S. Squash Racquets Association) patiently described the operations of their respective associations.

The other racquet games may not be as well known as the five major sports we focus on in this book, but they are just as fascinating and challenging. Pete Bostwick, the greatest amateur athlete I know, was particularly helpful with hard rackets and court tennis. Willie Surtees, the hard rackets champion, also gave much useful advice.

Gene Scott, who has dominated U.S. court tennis for years, lucidly analyzed court tennis strokes for me. Scott also arranged for me to use the splendid library of New York's Racquet and Tennis Club.

Bill Talbert, whose books are classics on tennis strategy, provided me with a matchless comparison of tennis and court tennis.

Former Wimbledon champion Chuck McKinley began by playing table tennis. His discussion of tennis and table tennis was unique.

Pedro Bacallao, the undisputed U.S. squash tennis champion, educated me in the tactics and techniques of his sport and frontennis.

Platform tennis and paddle tennis champions Hilary Hilton and Annabel Lang, ably abetted by paddle tennis sage Murray Geller, explained the East and West Coast versions of their sport.

Colonel Jim Anderson, director of physical education at the

U.S. Military Academy, contributed much advice on conditioning, as did Harry Hopman, the former Davis Cup coach for Australia.

The editors of *Tennis Magazine* and *Racquet* made it easy for me to study and talk with today's leading squash, badminton and racquetball players.

Finally, a double vote of thanks to my co-author, Jeff Bairstow. His scientific mind brought order out of chaos, and his creativity added fruit to what could have been a rather dry cereal.

New York City, 1979   Herb FitzGibbon

The Complete Racquet Sports Player

Chapter 1

What Is a Complete Racquet Sports Player?

The Universal Appeal of Racquet Games

For centuries man has found recreational pleasure in games that involve hitting a ball with a bat. There appears to be something innately pleasurable in the ability to make a ball fly through the air and, in so doing, defeating an opponent. The key is probably in that last phrase—"defeating an opponent." Many ball games developed because they provided exercise for warriors and gave them skills that were necessary in battle.

So it is hardly surprising that some ball games have become sports that produce warlike partisanship among players and spectators alike. Baseball in the United States and cricket in England are perhaps the two prime examples. Teams in these sports have a following just as avid as the crowds that cheered the Roman armies as they returned victorious from their foreign expeditions.

However, baseball and cricket are team sports that are practiced by relatively few members of the general public. Indeed, only the more dedicated amateurs continue to play beyond their school and college years. But just as baseball and cricket represent bat-and-ball games played between teams, so there are several varieties of bat-and-ball games between individuals. Such games are probably derived from hand-to-hand combat among primitive peoples. Indeed, the Aztecs played a racquet game from which the Basque game of pelota may have developed. The winner of the Aztec game, however, was allowed the head of his opponent. Racquet sports are still competitive but, fortunately, are not fought to the death.

In this century, the most popular of the individual bat-and-ball games have been the racquet sports—that is to say, the sports played with a strung racquet and a relatively small ball. Indeed, in the past decade, there has been unprecedented growth in the racquet sports in many countries. In the United States, tennis has boomed as a participant sport in recent years to the point where some estimates place the number of players as high as 30 million. In England and Australia, squash has become a popular sport during the past ten years or so.

What is significant is that the racquet sports are experiencing astounding growth as participant sports for people of all ages and of widely varying athletic prowess. Whereas baseball requires the ability either to throw or to hit a ball with considerable skill before much pleasure can be derived from the game as a player, the racquet sports seem to have a universal appeal to the beginning player whether young or old.

Quite obviously, all the racquet sports provide the immensely pleasurable feeling of hitting a ball with a bat or racquet and the opportunity to compete. However, there is something more to the racquet sports that does not exist in the simpler sports such as, say, swimming or skiing.

The racquet sports provide an endless variety of strokes and tactical situations that are never quite repeated. The player is constantly challenged by a ceaseless flow of shots and opportunities that are impossible to master totally for even the world's top-ranked players. No matter what the level of your play, you will never quite have the game under your complete control. Of course, there are days when a racquet sports player can put it all together and play at an unusually high level, but he will never achieve total mastery— and he will know that.

It is this constant challenge at any skill level that provides much of the universal appeal of the racquet sports. You do not have to be a Jimmy Connors or a Marty Hogan to experience the joys or frustrations of the racquet sports. A rank beginner can achieve as much satisfaction from batting a ball around a racquetball court as a country club tennis player might by winning his club's tournament.

This endless variety and constant challenge are common to all the racquet sports—badminton, platform tennis, racquetball, squash, tennis and all the variations of those games. They are all seemingly easy and yet often frustratingly difficult. At the same time, they are rarely boring for the participants, so that the players keep coming back for more and deriving even more pleasure as they meet one challenge after another. Not only do the racquet sports make demands on the players; they also provide rewards that all participants can feel.

Why Play More Than One Racquet Sport?

One of the purposes of this book is to encourage people who play one racquet sport to try the other racquet games. We think that not only will you enjoy a second or a third racquet sport but you will return to your original sport with a new and revived interest and understanding which may help you get more out of that sport, too.

You may have noticed that if you return to, say, tennis after a few weeks or months of abstinence, you play the first match at a remarkably high level despite your lack of recent practice. That's partly because your expectations of yourself are less so you play more loosely and without pressuring yourself. However, it's also because you are coming back to a game you enjoy and are rediscovering its pleasures. We feel that a second racquet sport can heighten that sense of awareness and so revive your interest in your first racquet sport.

That's a fairly subtle point, of course, and there are many other quite straightforward reasons for taking up another racquet sport. The simplest reason is that each of the five sports we're going to look at in some detail give a different kind of fun. If you play only one of these sports, you are missing out on some very enjoyable experiences. Sure, the racquet sports are competitive in nature, but they can all be played for purely social reasons. The Australians describe social tennis as "having a good hit," and we think you can do just that with all the racquet sports. You can have a good hit.

Another simple reason for playing more than one racquet sport is that in many places the games are of a seasonal nature. Despite the growth of indoor tennis courts, tennis is still largely a summer sport. That is why platform tennis was conceived—as a tennislike sport that could be played when the snow came. And despite the availability of air-conditioning, squash is largely a winter game. So the major racquet sports complement each other in terms of seasonality—you can play one in the summer months and another in the colder months.

By alternating sports in winter and summer you can get a real break from each sport so you will approach the next season's sport afresh and with renewed anticipation, as we suggested earlier. Of course, you can play two racquet sports in tandem throughout the year, but you will most likely find the continual switching back and forth much more difficult than making a complete changeover. We'll have more to say on this subject when we take a look at how to pick your sport in Chapter 3.

You may want to try a second racquet sport when you find that your first sport has become frustrating. Any racquet sports player knows that there are levels and plateaus within each sport. Trying to make the jump from one plateau to another can be intensely frustrating. That's the point where you should try another racquet sport. For example, many tennis players have found that racquetball is a very easy sport to pick up and have switched sports because they have reached a plateau in their tennis play. It's not uncommon for such racquetball converts to go back to tennis and find that they can now make an improvement in their game because of their new perspective. The same is true in reverse for keen racquetballers.

Each of the racquet sports provides different levels of physical activity. The game of doubles in tennis, while not necessarily very physically demanding at the amateur level, provides a mental challenge that many weekend players enjoy. On the other hand, singles in squash or racquetball will give an energetic workout for a player at almost any level. So if you are interested in improving your physical shape, you might want to try one of the more vigorous sports.

But whatever your own personal reasons might be, we think that you will find the overriding justification for playing several racquet sports to be that you'll find them all rewarding. If you find any satisfaction at all in hitting a ball with a racquet—and we assume you do or you would not be reading this book—then you will find all the racquet sports to be exhilarating, to be challenging and to be great fun to play.

Now, you probably think of yourself as a tennis player or a squash player or whatever. We hope that after reading this book you will want to be a racquet sports player—that is to say, one who plays more than one racquet sport. A complete racquet sports player is hard to find; we think that you might want to call yourself one when you can pick up a racquet and feel perfectly happy playing any of the five major racquet sports we concentrate on in this book.

To be a complete racquet sports player, you do not have to play all your sports at an advanced level, but you should have an understanding of each sport and its relationship to the other major racquet sports. In this book we have tried to detail those relationships by organizing it in a way that we hope will encourage you to become a complete racquet sports player. That is why subjects often don't come up in a predictable order; sometimes one sport leads a discussion in one chapter, but is placed last in another. There has been a method in our madness: the idea is to present *relationships* between one sport and another in the most intriguing fashion.

We hope this book will encourage you to become not just a tennis player or a racquetballer but to develop into a racquet sports player so that you are comfortable with and enjoy several racquet games. Both the authors have played the five major racquet sports (although at very different levels), so we intend to show that you can, too.

The Five Major Racquet Sports

We have chosen in this book to focus on the five major racquet sports—tennis, racquetball, badminton, squash and platform tennis for two reasons. First, these are the most popular racquet sports in terms of numbers of players. The other racquet sports, such as court tennis and paddle tennis, do have a loyal following —almost a fanatical one—but either are limited by a lack of facilities or do not show the potential for growth of the major racquet sports.

Second, the five sports that we will concentrate on seem to us to embody the essentials of a true racquet sport. One of them— platform tennis—is played with a paddle rather than a strung racquet, but it is a direct derivation of tennis. The games involve motion in three distinct areas: the movement of a racquet to hit a ball; the flight of a ball around a court whose limits are carefully prescribed; and the movement of players within that court.

Although table tennis is a very popular game, we have included it in this book only briefly because it seemed to us to be a different sport. It is played on a table and not within a walled or screened court; the dimensions of the table, net, ball and bat are much smaller, so the playing characteristics differ considerably from the other racquet sports; and the table tennis bat differs from strung racquets in its ability to put spins on the ball. No doubt these reasons will not please the devotees of table tennis, the game is so different in nature that we could not draw sufficient parallels to include a thorough discussion.

If you were to examine the five major racquet sports you would see that they are indeed closely related in many ways. Before we get down to the business of looking at the sports in some detail, it may be helpful to run quickly through the basic ideas behind each sport.

Let's start with *tennis,* by far the most popular and complicated of the big five. A simple definition of the game might say that two opponents face each other across a net and hit a ball back and forth over it with strung racquets. The objective of the game is to hit the ball so that your opponent does not return it over the net or in the court. That is obviously a much simplified description of a quite complicated game, but it will do for the moment.

Fig. 1. *The game of tennis*   *Tennis* magazine

Fig. 2. *The game of badminton*   Peter Lemon

    Badminton is a very close relative to tennis in that it is played on a court divided by a net. However, the players hit a feathered shuttlecock instead of a ball. The objective is much the same—to hit the shuttlecock in such a way that it cannot be returned over the net or in the court by the opponent. Of course, the shuttlecock will not bounce, unlike a tennis ball, so it must be kept in the air to remain in play.

22

Platform tennis, as you might expect from the name, is also a close relative of tennis. It was devised as a winter alternative to tennis and is played on a raised court from which the snow can be cleared easily. The court is much smaller than a tennis court but is divided by a net. The game is distinguished from tennis in several ways, but the most significant are that a paddle is used rather than a racquet, and the ball may be hit after it has bounced off the taut wire screens that surround the court. The latter introduces an entirely new element into the game for those who have previously played only conventional tennis.

Although their origins are quite different, there are similarities between platform tennis and the two walled court games that we are going to consider—squash and racquetball. They are all games in which the walls of the court play an important part. However, in squash and racquetball, the walls are everything—each ball that is hit must also strike the front wall. And unlike platform tennis, the opponents are not separated by a net.

Fig. 3. *The game of platform tennis* Amelia Island Plantation

Fig. 4. *The game of squash* *Racquet* magazine

In *squash*, both players face the same way and use a strung racquet to hit a rubber ball against the walls of a completely enclosed court. The objective here is to hit the ball so that it bounces off the front wall and cannot be satisfactorily returned by the opponent. The front wall has a small illegal area (the "telltale") near the floor which might almost be compared with the net of tennis. Balls hit into that area are out of play.

24

Racquetball is much like squash except that the players use a short-handled strung racquet and a larger, bouncier ball. The court is larger than for squash and, generally, is completely enclosed. All surfaces, including the ceiling, may be used for play. As with squash, the objective is to hit the ball against the front wall so that the opponent cannot make a satisfactory return. There is no telltale that must be cleared.

So there are clearly links between each of the five major racquet sports in terms of the objectives of the game, the equipment used and the playing courts. Fortunately, these links are such that a player can quite easily move from one sport to another, but the differences are sufficiently great to guarantee that competence in one racquet sport does not automatically lead to competence in another.

Fig. 5. *The game of racquetball*   World International Racquets Championships/Bristol-Myers/Vitalis

A few years ago, five world champions in their respective racquet sports were pitted against each other in the sports each did not ordinarily play. The winner of this, perhaps artificial, contest was a squash champion, Sharif Khan, who turned out to be the only one of the five champions who had prior experience in most of the other racquet sports, having played them in high school or college. However, the other contestants, such as Bjorn Borg, the tennis star, and Charlie Brumfield, the racquetball champion, all agreed that they had relished the opportunity to try the other racquet sports but had no idea they could be so demanding.

What was obvious from watching these great athletes play an unfamiliar sport was that the patterns of stroking and strategy of one racquet sport cannot easily be translated into another racquet sport. The purpose of this book is to help you make those adaptations so that you can take what you already know from one racquet sport and use it to help you get the most from a second sport.

Chapter 2

The Elements of Racquet Sports Play

An Introduction to the Racquet Sports

We hope that this chapter will give you a feel for each of our five major racquet sports—tennis, badminton, platform tennis, squash and racquetball. We will take a brief look at each of the sports in terms of the nature of the game itself, the strokes and strategies required and what the intending player should bring to a new sport.

If you are already familiar with any of the five sports we are about to discuss, you'll probably find the explanations rather basic and oversimplified. Please bear with us—you may find it easier simply to skip the sport you already know so well. If you have a basic grasp of all five sports, just skip this entire chapter.

Following this chapter, we'll get into the grips, serves and stroking techniques for each sport in rather more detail. We'll also take a more thorough look at strategy, equipment and conditioning for the racquet sports. We'll suggest some ways for you to pick your next racquet sport—how to find the sport that will suit your style and personality, so to speak.

If, in reading this chapter, you think that we have not gone far enough in our explanations, you can probably find the material you want in later chapters or in the rules of each sport given in the Appendix. However, we would caution you against reading the rules until you have played the sport. Should that sound strange to you, think about it this way: the best way to pick up a new racquet sport is to go out and do it with a player who is already familiar with the sport. A player can get you going and tell you all you need to know about the rules as you play. The rules that we have included are for reference, and we hope that you'll treat them that way.

If you find that you need to know more about the racquet sports we describe, we have attempted to simplify that for you by including a brief bibliography following the last chapter. These are the books that we have enjoyed on each of the sports and we think you will, too.

Having said all that, let us now turn to the main business of this chapter—the basic elements of each of our five major racquet sports. We are starting with tennis because that is the most popular racquet sport of the moment and likely to be so for many years. We are following with the other sports by design, not in order of popularity but because each bears some common relation to the preceding one. So although we end with racquetball, this does not indicate its standing in any way in terms of either the sport's popularity or the authors' own prejudices.

Tennis: A Game of Steadiness

Tennis is the slowest of the five major racquet sports largely because it is played on the largest court (Figure 6), so the ball has to travel the greatest distances. The size of the court and the great variety of shots make tennis the most difficult of all our five racquet sports. Tennis is a game where consistency is at a premium. Most tennis matches are won or lost on errors, not on

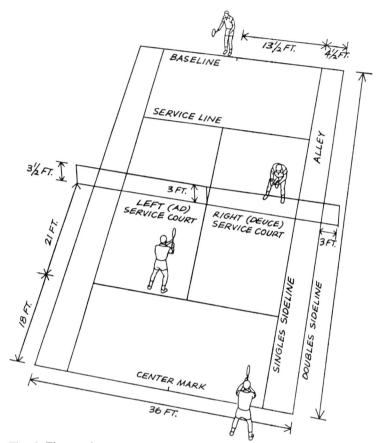

Fig. 6. *The tennis court*

winning shots. In other words, the number of errors in a match will far outnumber the winners. Consequently, the player who makes the fewest errors will usually win a tennis match.

So tennis requires a fundamental grounding in strokes. A tennis player must have a wide repertoire of strokes and, ideally, should be able to hit those strokes off either side of his body. He should be able to hit the ball after it has bounced (the ground stroke) or before it bounces (the volley); he should be able to put the ball in

29

play (serve) consistently; and he should be able to hit the ball in the air with an overhead motion (the smash). He should also be able to hit gentle, touch shots when the occasion demands. And when a tennis player's game goes sour, it is to his stroking that a player will usually look first.

Frequently, the caliber of a player's strokes will determine his strategy. A player who does not have a powerful serve and lacks confidence in volleying will prefer to stay in the backcourt and trade shots with his opponent until one of them makes an error. A player with a good serve and accurate volleys will often close in on the net, hoping to end the point with an aggressive winning volley. Both types of player can be successful. Chris Evert and Bjorn Borg have games that are largely played from the baseline. Arthur Ashe and Martina Navratilova favor an attacking style with much net play.

Conditioning is not usually a deciding factor in tennis for the average player, especially for the doubles version of the game. However, tennis does involve a great deal of rapid movement around the court, so some fast footwork is necessary. Thus, tennis players need to be quick off the mark and should be able to move rapidly either laterally or forward and back. Tennis calls for very short bursts of concentrated activity with periodic rests between games.

Equipment can be significant in tennis play, especially the choice of racquet and the way that it is strung. We'll have more to say about equipment in a later chapter, but for now we'll note that racquets, balls and shoes are all important for proper tennis performance. And although clothes play a lesser part in determining the quality of play, tennis players, historically, have paid more attention to their clothes than other racquet sports players. So the choice of clothes can be important to a player.

For a newcomer to tennis, one of the major drawbacks, aside from the complexity and difficulty of the strokes, is the arcane scoring system. However, it is this system that gives a tennis match a particular flavor and can cause the match to ebb or flow in one player's favor within the course of a few points. Although attempts have been made to change the scoring, alternative methods lose this important quality even though they may gain in terms of spectator understanding.

Briefly, a tennis match is scored in sets, the first player to win two sets winning the match (in a few men's singles tournaments, the first player to win three sets). A set is won by the first player to win six games, provided that he has a margin of two games. If the players reach six-games-all, a tie-breaker game is played with special scoring for that game. It is the scoring of individual games that gives most novices a few problems.

In a match, a flip of a coin or spin of a racquet determines which player can choose to serve or receive first. The server serves all the points of the first game, and the serve alternates after each game is completed, irrespective of who wins the previous game. Either server or receiver may score points. The first point is called "15," the second "30" and the third "40." The player who scores the point beyond 40 wins the game unless the score is tied at 40-all (called "deuce" in tennis jargon). In that case, one player has to further score two consecutive points to win the game. The first point after deuce is called "advantage" —if for the server, it is "advantage-in" or more simply "ad-in"; if for the receiver, it is "advantage-out" or "ad-out." In a closely contested game, the score may return to deuce several times as one player or the other fails to get the two-point margin to close out the game.

It is this two-point margin in games, and similarly the two-game lead required to win a set, that gives a tennis player a "second chance." It is considerably harder to get two points in a row or two games in a row than one point or one game. This leads to some unusual pressures for the players.

Badminton: Deception and Attrition

To those who have never played the game or never watched a top-class match, badminton often has the reputation of a "sissy" sport. Nothing could be further from the truth. Badminton is the fastest of the racquet sports. The game requires the participants to be in excellent physical shape. Although the equipment is light and the court (Figure 7) is smaller than for tennis, a badminton match can be much more strenuous than tennis. Badminton players not only have to be quick off the mark but should have considerable stamina for competitive play. In fact, badminton is so demanding that it is almost a game of attrition, where the objective is to tire the opponent and so win the match.

But conversely, badminton is not a slam-bang game. Many

Fig. 7. *The badminton court*

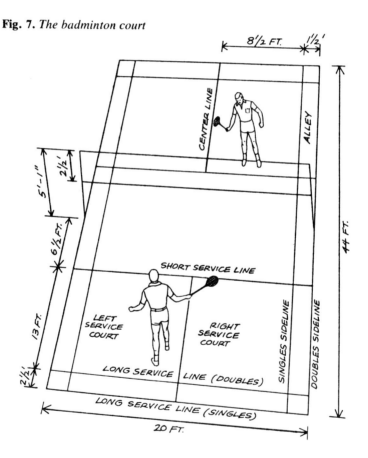

badminton shots call for precise touch and timing because the equipment is so light that a slight turn of the wrist will produce a large change of direction. The flight of the shuttlecock is quite unlike that of a ball. The "bird" can move very rapidly through the air and then drop agonizingly slowly, giving a receiver time to set up for the return. Or the bird can be flicked gently over the net to die before the opponent can race up to retrieve the point. So badminton also calls for considerable skill in shotmaking.

However, the basics of badminton are relatively easy to learn, so any racquet sports player can soon pick up the rudiments of the game. While badminton is perhaps easier to learn than tennis, the two sports are very similar in that there are plateaus of skill. Making the jump from one level to the next can be extremely difficult and frustrating. Like tennis, badminton demands considerable attention to stroking in order to rise to a higher level of play, but generally technique is less important to the enjoyment of badminton than for tennis.

In a badminton match, the server serves diagonally, as in tennis, but from a position close to the net instead of from the baseline (see Chapter 5). However, the serve must be hit with an underarm motion, and the server is permitted only one attempt. Thus the badminton serve is not the attacking weapon of the tennis serve. It is possible to win the point with a badminton serve, but this is very rare among better players.

Possession of the serve is important, however, since only the server can score points. If the server hits a fault or otherwise loses the point, the serve passes to his opponent, who then serves until he loses a point. So the server can score a run of points as long as he retains the serve.

In singles play particularly, the objective of the game is to move the opponent around the court as much as possible and to try to force him to hit the bird up. If one player hits it up, his opponent will then have the chance to close in on the net and smash the bird back down and so win the point. So the overhead smash is a vital shot for badminton.

Because the bird may never bounce and the net is five feet high in the center, most badminton shots are hit over the head. We have just noted the importance of the overhead smash but equally important is the overhead "clear," which is a defensive shot used to hit the bird high in the air for the full length of the court. A clear has the function of the tennis lob in that it will force an opponent away from the midcourt, where he can attack, to the backcourt, where he will usually hit a defensive return.

The doubles version of badminton is considerably less demanding than singles. With two players to cover the court, there is less movement, but on the other hand, more skill is required to place the bird where it will be the most difficult to return. Men's doubles is usually played with a side-by-side formation on defense and a one-up, one-back formation for attack. In mixed doubles, the woman usually covers the net and the man the backcourt, so mixed is a different game from single-sex doubles.

The choice of shuttlecock is important. There are several weights of bird and shapes of feathers. The feathers may be natural or synthetic. Novices often use birds that are too slow, which makes for a slow and defensive game.

Clothing for serious indoor badminton is usually white, and good tennis clothes are acceptable.

The scoring of badminton is relatively simple. A match is won by the first side to win two games. A game may be either 11 points (women's singles) or 15 points (doubles and men's singles). A minor complication may arise when the score reaches 13-all in a 15-point game. At this stage, the score may be "set" by the team that first reaches 13. This means that the first team to win a further 5 points will win the game. A game can also be set to 3 points at 14-all. Or, of course, the sides can decline to set and simply play to 15.

Platform Tennis: A Cat-and-Mouse Game

In many ways, platform tennis is a hybrid racquet sport—it has some of the virtues of a net-court sport like badminton and tennis, and it has some of the virtues of an enclosed-court sport like squash and racquetball, since the ball can be taken on the rebound from the wire screens (see Figure 8). But the major difference between platform tennis and the other major racquet sports is that virtually all play is doubles. Singles is generally played informally and that very occasionally. This concentration on doubles is no accident—the inventors of the sport were looking for a game with the sociability of tennis that could be played outdoors in the winter. Much platform tennis play is still of this variety—a social game played in bracing weather. The singles version has several disadvantages for the average player due to the small size of the court.

Since a platform court is half the dimensions of a tennis court, control of the net is essential. Thus, the object of the game is to go to the net and to stay there until the point is won. A server will always follow his serve to the net to maintain the all-important net position. The receiver will return the ball aggressively in the hope of preventing the server from getting to a good net position. Likewise, the receiving team will use all the means at its disposal to get the serving team away from the net so they can claim the controlling position for themselves.

Only one serve is permitted in platform play, so a reliable spin serve is a must, but a flat serve will be adequate for a novice. Power is not vital, since a serve that is hit too hard will rebound from the wire screens, giving the receiver plenty of time to make an effective and often attacking return. However, placement of the serve is important (see Chapter 5).

A platform tennis player should have a variety of shots, although it is not essential to be equally good off both sides: most players have strong forehands and will run around a weaker backhand much of the time. A well-controlled lob is essential and is used more frequently than in the other racquet sports. That means the overhead smash is also a vital part of the platform player's game. These shots are more compact than the tennis swing and so are easier to learn for the novice player. And, of course, the paddle is shorter than a tennis racquet, so most players find ball contact much easier.

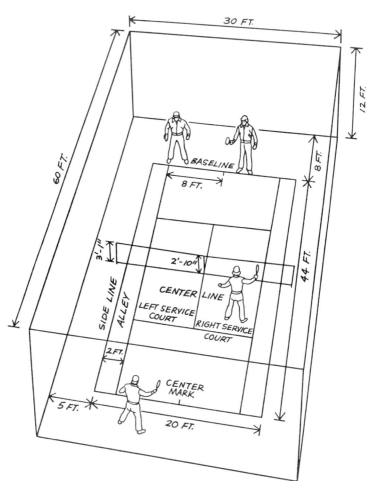

Fig. 8. *The platform tennis court*

Since much of the play is at the net, there is a premium on quick and accurate volleys. Although footwork is quite important, hand quickness is the key. The volleys must be hit without changing grips and with an almost reflex action. Unlike footwork, hand quickness is lost only slowly with increasing age, so former tennis players often do well at platform play. Two current examples are Clark Graebner and one of the authors (HSFG).

Converts from the enclosed-court sports will probably have little difficulty in adapting to the rebound shots of platform tennis. However, tennis players often find the screen shots confusing. A tennis player will tend to play the ball before it gets to the screens instead of waiting with his racquet back ready to follow the ball as it comes off the wires. Screen play is one of the peculiar delights of platform tennis, but it does require practice to develop the patience and timing to return effectively.

As in tennis, platform tennis matches are generally won on errors: the side making the fewest errors will win. So steadiness is a virtue in platform play. Since the screens can prevent a team from being overpowered by hard-hit shots, much restraint is needed to wait for the winning opportunity. Teamwork is very important in setting up a winning situation. Good teamwork calls for constant communication and discussion of tactics when the game is going badly.

The scoring of platform tennis is exactly like that of tennis (except for tie-breakers), and the playing rules are generally the same except for the single serve and the use of the screens (see rules in Appendix).

Platform tennis equipment is very simple. The paddles are usually of wood, although fiberglass and aluminum are also used. The balls are of solid sponge rubber, colored yellow or orange. Because the platform is covered with an abrasive surface (to aid the players' traction), the balls tend to wear out very quickly. The abrasive surface also takes its toll of shoes, which should have hard-wearing soles and be well cushioned to prevent blisters. Clothing is traditionally very casual—comfortable and warm is the usual style, although tennis clothes are often worn in warmer areas.

Squash: Fast and Furious

The game of squash—or more correctly "squash racquets," since the game is a derivative of the English game of rackets—is perhaps the toughest physically of our five major racquet sports. A half hour of squash is probably equal to three or more sets of tennis in terms of the exercise obtained and the calories expended. Until recently, the game was difficult to learn because the novice often had problems hitting the hard rubber ball with a sufficiently powerful stroke to make it bounce. However, the advent of a new softer, bouncier ball (the 70+ ball, so-called because it is tested at 70° Fahrenheit) will undoubtedly encourage the further spread of squash.

There are two distinct versions of the game of squash—the North American and the British or International game. The British game uses softer balls and is played on a court that is two and a half feet wider than the U.S. court. The rules also differ markedly. Consequently, points in the international game are considerably longer and require a greater repertoire of shots. Naturally, the British feel that their game is superior, but one top U.S. player has described the game as being akin to "whacking a dead mouse around the court with a wet mop." Be that as it may, we will concentrate on the North American game, which is the one commonly found on this side of the Atlantic.

Due to the confined nature of the squash court (Figure 9) and the vigorous style of play, singles is the preferred version of the sport. Although doubles can be and is played at the tournament level, most novices will play only singles. In singles, the key is to stay in front of your opponent, preferably by returning to the "T" formed by the lines marking the two service courts. From the T position almost all shots can be reached.

The squash serve is a lob-like finesse shot designed to keep the

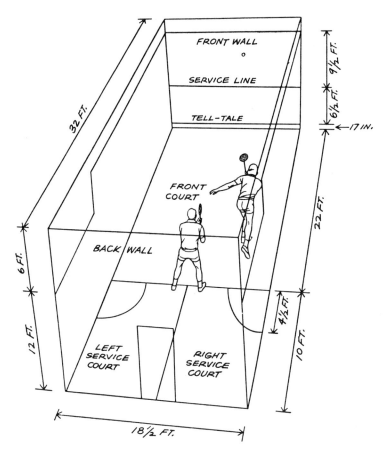

Fig. 9. *The squash court*

receiver deep and away from the center of the court. The serve is hit alternately from each side of the court to rebound off the front wall into the opposite service court (see Chapter 5). The squash player should have a variety of serves to keep his opponent guessing. The return of serve is almost always defensive, since the receiver will usually be deep in the backcourt.

Stroking technique is important in squash but perhaps not quite as much as in tennis because you need only hit the front wall instead of clearing the net into the opposite court. A squash player should be equally competent off both sides from deep in the court. The volley is not used much in North American squash, although tennis players who are used to volleying will find the ability useful in squash. However, the lob is a useful stroke in squash. Lobs are often hit down the sidewalls where they are difficult to return without the racquet hitting the wall.

Most of the shots in squash are hit with considerable wrist snap to get extra pace on the ball. Underspin is used so the ball will drop off the front wall, while sidespin is often used for deception and control. Many shots have to be made below the knees, since one of the objectives of the game is to keep the ball low. However, the ball cannot be "killed," as in racquetball, because the court is smaller and a low shot to the front wall will often hit the telltale or "tin" and so be out of play. The tell-tale is a strip of sheet metal 17 inches wide across the bottom of the front wall. It is this feature of squash that makes for longer and more interesting rallies in the more advanced levels of the game. It is harder to put the ball away completely than in racquetball.

Footwork is more important in squash and racquetball than in tennis and platform tennis. Players must be capable of making sudden starts and stops, so muscles should be quite flexible. Torn Achilles tendons are not uncommon among unfit squash players. So warm-up exercises are advisable for occasional or older players. Like badminton, squash is very nearly a continuous game which calls for considerable stamina. Most squash players feel that playing the game is sufficient exercise for building stamina, and this may be true for frequent players. Weekend players may have to build their stamina by running or other exercise.

In the North American version, the first player to reach 15 points wins the game unless the score is tied at 13-all or 14-all. At 13-all the score may be set 5 or 3 points as in badminton. At 14-all, the score may be set 3 points. The player who wins three games wins the match. The order of serving is decided by spinning a racquet, and the first server continues to serve until he loses a point. Unlike the international game, points may be scored by either server or receiver. The service rules for the international game are considerably more complicated, and we won't go into them here.

Squash racquets are usually all wood, although metal and fiberglass have been used. Stringing may be gut or nylon, although stringing is not as critical a factor as with a tennis racquet. Clothing is usually as for tennis, with white preferred in most clubs. Squash clubs are traditionally very conservative and may enforce an all-white dress code. Shoes should be comfortable and well-padded. Two pairs of socks are advisable to reduce the chance of blisters from the rapid starts and stops.

Racquetball: The Simple Power Game

The newest of our five racquet sports, racquetball, is already the second most popular game in our grouping. That's largely because the game is easy to learn, simple to play and gives a good workout to the players in a short space of time. The principles and strokes of racquetball are much like those of squash, but the court (Figure 10) is larger, the racquets are shorter and more manageable, and the balls are bigger and bouncier. All this adds up to a game that anyone who has ever handled a racquet before can learn in a half hour or so and be playing quite competently after only a few sessions. So it is hardly surprising that racquetball has boomed in the past few years, especially among women.

Curiously enough, although the game is simple for beginners and has long rallies, at the top amateur and professional level racquetball is generally a game of power shots with very short rallies. However, we are concerned with racquetball as a participant sport—and a very satisfying sport it is for players at the club level.

As in squash, control of the center court is the key to racquetball play. The server will attempt to keep the receiver deep in the

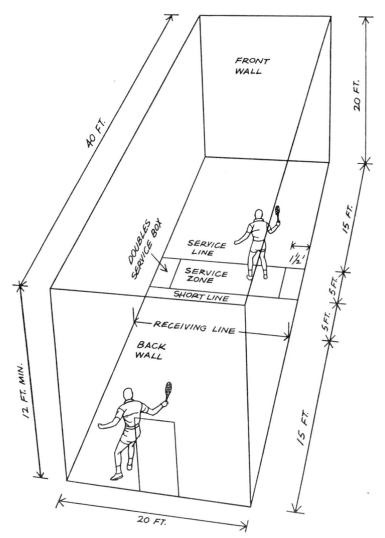

Fig. 10. *The racquetball court*

backcourt while waiting for a low ball that can be pounded low to the front wall—the "kill" shot—and be unreturnable on the rebound. Unlike squash, there is no telltale on a racquetball court's front wall, so the ball can be hit very low, provided that it does not hit the floor before getting to the front wall.

Most racquetball is singles play for the same reasons as in squash—four players flailing around the court are a danger to each other and themselves—so we'll concentrate on the singles version of the sport. We'll also stick to the four-wall, totally enclosed court game, although racquetball in some parts of the United States is played outdoors on one- and three-wall courts. The type that most players will encounter is the four-wall game.

As in squash, a racquetball server continues to serve as long as he is winning points, but he is not required to serve alternately to different halves of the court, nor must the serve be hit above a certain height on the front wall (see Chapter 5). However, a server should have a variety of serves and be able to place them well. Power is not really necessary for a good serve; in fact, a serve that is hit too hard and high will bounce off the back wall giving the receiver a relatively easy opportunity to return.

Once the ball has been served legally, the players may use all four walls of the court and the ceiling in the course of a rally. A common return is the "ceiling" ball, which is a lob-like shot preferably hit down one of the sidewalls so that it touches the ceiling a few feet ahead of the front wall. Players may hit a succession of ceiling balls waiting for the chance to get a low ball that can be killed against the front wall to close out the point.

The small, loosely strung racquet encourages big swings with pronounced wrist snap at impact. Strokes are similar to those in squash but with little or no spin. Many racquetballers have strong forehands and weak backhands. At the lower levels of the game it is often possible to run around a weaker backhand, but ideally players should be competent off both sides.

Most kill shots are hit when a player is in front of his opponent. When presented with a low ball in the backcourt, a player will often hit a "pass" shot—a low drive that will rebound deep into the backcourt—in the hope of getting the opponent away from the center court position and gaining that position for himself. Kills, pass shots and ceiling balls form the basis of the racquetballer's game, but there are many other shots with very distinctive names (racquetball has a reputation for uninhibited play and jargon). We'll get to those shots in later chapters.

Scoring for racquetball is quite simple. A game is won by the first player to reach 21 points, and the first player to win two games wins the match. Under U.S. Racquetball Association rules, a tie-breaker game of 11 points is played if the score reaches one-game-all. However, this rule is under discussion and may change shortly.

Racquetball play is very demanding physically and play is continuous with the exception of player-requested "time-outs" in tournament play. Professional racquetballers use these time-outs and equipment time-outs to psych their opponents at critical points in the game by destroying the rhythm of a scoring streak. Racquetball is a vigorous game and quite rowdy by comparison with the more decorous game of tennis. However, to many afficionados, this is one of the appealing points of the sport.

Until recently, clothing has also been uninhibited on the court. However, as the sport matures, this is beginning to change and clothing is becoming more sophisticated, as are racquets and the quality of the balls.

Chapter 3

How to Pick Your Sport

You Are Not Alone

The mere fact that you are reading this book suggests you have a pretty strong desire to try more than one racquet sport, or maybe you have already tried a couple. Although devotees of a particular racquet sport tend to advocate their own choice with a fervor bordering on religious fanaticism, there is no need to feel guilty about tiring of one sport and wanting to try another. It is one of our most favorable national characteristics that we pursue novelty at almost any expense. So why not in racquet sports?

We have found that there are significant numbers of amateurs who can and do play more than one racquet sport. Many platform tennis players are avid tennis players in the summer season. A good many squash players indulge in a little tennis, too, during the summer months. And it's rare to find a badminton player who has never lifted a tennis racquet at some stage in his or her sports career.

You will have noticed that tennis is often the favored alternate sport for many racquet sports players. There are many reasons for this, of course, not the least being that tennis has become very popular, and facilities exist if not in profusion at least in sufficient quantity in most parts of the country. And tennis is a complementary summer game to those racquet sports that are traditionally played in the winter months. Many of the other racquet sports were developed as winter substitutes for tennis.

So, if you find yourself hankering after another racquet sport, you are not alone; others have done exactly the same thing (and frequently with very satisfying results). The question then arises, of course, of which sport to choose. Just how do you decide on the racquet sport that you should try next? That is the purpose of this chapter—to give you a few ideas that will help your decision-making. Since we do not know your athletic ability, we cannot, as it were, prescribe the racquet sport that will fit your personality and be compatible with your lifestyle. You'll have to make those judgments for yourself. All we can do is give you some rather general, but we hope useful, advice.

Racquetball: A Beginner's Sport

If you have never tried the sport, we suggest you try racquetball simply because it is an easy game to start playing and a couple of sessions will be enough to tell you if you have an aptitude for it. Not that we are saying racquetball is a sport that you will master quickly. None of the racquet sports are that simple. No, we mean racquetball has the right combination of court, racquet and ball for virtually anyone to have fun within 10 or 15 minutes of stepping inside a court for the very first time. Racquetball is a game that is loaded with thrills at every level of competence. That is why the sport has grown from 50,000 participants in 1970 to an estimated six million plus today.

Racquetball is the easiest of the major racquet sports because the racquet is just a very short (18 inches) extension of the hand with a large hitting surface (11 inches long by 9 inches wide). By comparison, the average tennis racquet is more than 26 inches long with a hitting surface that is not much larger than a racquetball racquet. In fact, tennis racquet designs are now getting much bigger in response to the needs of the average player. So hitting a racquetball is not much harder than hitting a ball with the palm of your hand. Not surprisingly, the dimensions and rules of racquetball are derived from those of handball and paddleball, and many handballers and paddleballers have become fine racquetball players. Charlie Brumfield, the former national racquetball champion, won several paddleball titles before he turned to racquetball (where he had even greater success).

Not only is the racquet easy to handle, but the ball is extremely lively, allowing the player plenty of time to get to it before it bounces a second time. Thus, not much physical strength is required to hit the ball to the front wall in such a way that it will bounce in the backcourt. Indeed, too much power in a beginner can be a distinct problem, since the ball will bounce all over the court, like a billiard ball caroming around a pool table, usually leaving an easy setup for the opponent.

Finally, the strokes of racquetball are not very complicated, since the objective of the game is quite simple—to hit the ball against quite a large front wall (20 feet by 20 feet) without the hindrance of a net. Unlike squash, all of the racquetball court (even the ceiling) may be used in an attempt to get the ball to bounce off the front wall. So the objectives of the game are easily understood by the beginner.

Racquetball has only three main strokes—forehand and backhand drives and the overhead or ceiling ball (see Chapter 6 for more details on these strokes). The serve is so similar to the forehand drive that the two can almost be considered to be one stroke. The serve is slightly simpler in that the ball is dropped and hit, providing an easier and slower-moving target. Although all these strokes use a full swing, muscular strength is not a prerequisite to generating power. Wrist snap is the key to producing power. Any squash or badminton player will be accustomed to using the wrist to generate power, but tennis players used to keeping a firm wrist sometimes have difficulty snapping it.

Racquetball has been described as wind sprints with a racquet. There is some truth in the statement. Although the distances covered on a racquetball court are not as great as in tennis, the movements are quicker and the game is often far more energetic. While playing an hour of tennis in the hot sun may sap your strength, the sport really does very little for your cardiovascular system. By contrast, an hour of racquetball—if you can last that long—is tremendous exercise, great fun and far less demanding mentally than tennis. You can really let it all hang out and get rid of your aggressions (and inhibitions, too) in a way that would never be possible on a tennis court.

So racquetball is the ideal game to try out quickly (assuming that there are facilities in your area), but that's not to say the other racquet sports ought to be ignored, so let's consider the others—not in any particular order.

Platform Tennis: A Concentrated Tennis Game

If you have ever played tennis, especially if you are a frustrated tennis player, you should try platform tennis, a sport that has many of the virtues of its larger sister and fewer of its vices. Like racquetball, platform tennis is an energetic game, but the distances covered are less than in any other of the major racquet sports—because the court is smaller and the game is played only in the doubles version—so the players will not end up completely wiped out after an hour or so's play.

Not only is the playing area of a platform court small, but the court is surrounded by wire screens that are designed to return the balls, so very little time is wasted in going after stray ones. The size, the screens and the proximity of not only your partner but also your opponents lead to some very concentrated play. Working in a confined area with your partner is like the interplay between opponents in squash and racquetball but is more satisfying because you are working with your partner rather than against an opponent. This teamwork is an essential component of platform tennis. Although tennis doubles is similar to platform in objectives, the large size of a tennis court does not give the intimacy of platform play. You and your partner will have to form a real team if you are to be at all successful.

And yet, in spite of the closeness of the platform court, you will have a feeling of space since the game is played outdoors. Neither squash nor racquetball can provide that sublime feeling of being in contact with the elements. And, of course, much platform play is in the winter months, when the cold temperatures and, as often happens in the Northeast, the sight of snow all around can give you a sense of exhilaration comparable only to skiing. No other racquet sport can provide this feeling.

In actual play, platform tennis can be compared with racquetball. The wooden paddle is short (17 inches) and has a relatively large hitting area (9 inches by 8 inches). So the paddle is like an extension of your hand. The court is quite small, so power does not count for as much as in conventional tennis. Thus platform is easier to play than tennis. The strokes are similar to those of tennis, often requiring a full swing with a firm wrist. However, the backhand, that bane of many weekend tennis players, is not quite so vital in platform play. In fact, many platform players just lob off the backhand side or run around to hit a forehand. The results seem to work out fine in either case.

Movement on the platform court consists of short, quick steps. The area is quite small and you will have a partner to cover his or her side of the court, so you will not need the conditioning of either squash, racquetball or tennis. Nevertheless, on a sharp winter's day, a few sets of platform play can provide a fine workout that will leave you tired but exhilarated.

If tennis can be described as long-range warfare, platform tennis is probably street fighting. You will often find yourself defending shots aimed at your midsection from a mere ten feet away. Consequently, fast reflexes and good racquet instincts are essential to survival on the platform court.

Unlike tennis, perfect form is not needed for quite adequate platform play. If you have reasonable hand-eye coordination, you will be able to make a stab at platform tennis. However, to improve, proper technique is essential. And that, as in tennis, requires work. Platform tennis will, of course, repay you in the form of a higher level of play. Like tennis, platform has plateaus of play, and one of the challenges of the sport is moving from one to the next.

Tennis: The Everest of the Racquet Sports

If you'd like to be considered a complete racquet sports player, tennis is a must. And yet, it must be admitted, tennis is not an easy sport either to learn or to play. In fact, tennis is so difficult that we would call it the Everest of the racquet sports—it poses the highest challenges and offers the most frustrations of any of the major racquet sports. So why do we advocate playing this almost unsurmountable game?

Well, like Everest, because it is there. The sport poses a series of challenges that few amateur sportsmen can resist. After all, it looks easy when a player gets it all together. The strokes have a fluid quality that can appear extremely graceful. The mental aspects are enough to challenge the most intellectual of players. And, above all, tennis is a gladiatorial competition—opponents can be satisfactorily vanquished.

The satisfactions of tennis are as abundant as the challenges. Played outdoors on a bright, sparkling summer's day with breezes rippling the nearby trees, tennis has a feeling of openness, of freedom that is rarely matched by any other sport, whether individual or team. You are unencumbered by walls or opponents. Even the traditional tennis whites suggest a crisp purity that is in its own way satisfying.

However, you will quickly realize that tennis is, indeed, the summit of the racquet sports because it is so difficult. Nonetheless, even if you don't make it to the top (and very few players get anywhere near) there is an innate pleasure in trying, just as the mountain climber will enjoy a 50-foot rock face even though he knows that Everest is out of his reach. There are enough small pleasures in a game of tennis to make it more than worthwhile for the 30 million players in the United States today.

If you have never tried tennis, consider the following: to conquer the game you must put in endless hours of practice for at least five years; there are seven variations on the forehand (high, low, deep, short, approach, pass and return of serve); likewise for the backhand; there are at least half a dozen different varieties of serve; then you should possess an overhead, a lob and a drop shot, to say nothing of the more advanced strokes that have a useful place in the tennis player's repertoire; and then there are tactics and strategy.

If all this isn't enough, you must learn to play on different surfaces and to put up with the widely varying elements of sun and wind while trying to hit a hard ball with a heavy racquet. Is it any wonder that we call tennis the Everest of the racquet sports?

The list of good tennis players who have quit the sport and become successful in another sport is legion. For example, Vic Niederhoffer, who dominated U.S. squash for almost a decade, was a varsity tennis player at Harvard but was no standout in Ivy League play (in itself not the summit of college tennis). However, Niederhoffer took up squash during his freshman year and became the top college squash player after only four seasons. Not only was he successful in squash, but with little or no experience in competitive racquetball, Niederhoffer reached the quarterfinals of the national racquetball championships on his first (and only) attempt. There are many other examples of players who switched from tennis to other racquet sports. However, there are no examples of top players turning to tennis and achieving national prominence.

Nonetheless, tennis can be a satisfying game, even at the lower levels, provided that you as a player recognize your limitations. Many older players enjoy a form of tennis that would be abhorred by a pair of 20-year-old hotshots. More than any other racquet sport, tennis is a game of levels of play. If you can be happy at a certain level of play, tennis can truly be a lifetime sport. But if you become dissatisfied with your level, it's time to move on to another racquet sport.

Badminton: An Unfamiliar Old Friend

No doubt you have played badminton at least once in your childhood—the old backyard or beach version of the game with a droopy net and dime-store equipment. So much of badminton is familiar to many racquet sports players. But real badminton is as far removed from the backyard variety as a walk in the park is from a climb of a Himalayan peak. The indoor game with the correct equipment is as tough and demanding physically as any of the racquet sports. It is almost as challenging to learn and develop competency as tennis. And the rewards are certainly comparable with those of any other racquet sport.

While it is relatively easy to begin hitting the badminton shuttlecock and even to rally comfortably, the sport has definite plateaus of competence just like those of tennis. And, as in tennis, hard work and practice are required to climb from one level to the next. Badminton can be a game of speed and lightning-fast returns. It can also be a game that calls for extremes of touch and changes of pace. Some fast footwork will be needed, such that top-flight badminton could be the most strenuous of any of the racquet sports.

If you have played one of the more wristy racquet sports such as racquetball or squash, you will find the transition to badminton relatively easy. Badminton strokes, while often quite simple, often require excessive wrist action to generate shuttle speed and to disguise the direction of the shot. Tennis players used to hitting a ball with a firm wrist will find badminton strokes relatively undisciplined. However, tennis players will quickly appreciate the basic strategy of badminton, which is to be in position to hit down on the shuttle when possible.

Racquet control is a vital part of badminton play. It is not easily learned for players accustomed to heavier racquets and heavier balls. Grips are important in proper stroking (see Chapter 4) except close to the net. So badminton is not a game that can be picked up quickly like racquetball. Yet, the game will repay effort in the same way that practice pays off for the dedicated tennis player.

Squash: A Changing Game

Squash has had limited growth in the United States, partly because the facilities are expensive to construct and partly because it is one of the harder racquet sports to learn. However, squash is now moving out of the private club atmosphere and is easier to learn, thanks to the new, bouncier 70+ ball. Nonetheless, squash poses more initial difficulty than our other major racquet sports unless you have already played racquetball (a similar sport but no relative).

The stroking skills of squash lie somewhere between those of racquetball and tennis. Like racquetball, squash requires a limited number of strokes, Unlike racquetball, those strokes are often difficult to master sufficiently to play adequately. The strokes are tougher to execute because the racquet is not merely an extension of the hand. The squash racquet is 27 inches long with a small hitting surface (8½ inches long by 8 inches wide). In fact, the squash racquet has the worst ratio of hitting surface to length among the major racquet sports. Thus racquet control is hard to achieve in squash without extensive practice. And practice for the beginner is tough because the ball still bounces like a rotten orange compared with a racquetball or a tennis ball. So some significant level of skill is needed even to practice by rallying with yourself in squash.

However, for the racquetballer, squash is the logical alternative because of the similarities of court, strokes and strategies. Squash may also provide more of a challenge to the accomplished racquetballer, as the longer racquet makes hitting the smaller, deader ball more difficult. Further, the smaller court increases the chance of physical contact significantly, making correct court movement a necessity. Racquetballers will find squash a challenge, although not quite so insurmountable as tennis.

Tennis players who are looking for a winter alternative will also find squash an intriguing racquet sport. Squash will provide much more of a workout in the winter months than a game of tennis doubles (or even singles) on an indoor tennis court. However, tennis players and racquetballers may find the restrictions of squash hard to live with at first. Squash is a game of both power and precision—two qualities that often have to be traded off for the novice player. However, squash is fun, with a little more style than racquetball, which makes it appeal to the more traditional tennis player.

A Few Final Thoughts

If all the foregoing sounds unbearably complicated, here are some simple suggestions, without any justifications. These ideas represent the authors' own view of the affinities of each of the major racquet sports.

If you are a tennis player, try platform tennis.
If you are a platform tennis player, try badminton.
If you are a badminton player, try tennis.
If you are a racquetballer, try squash.
If you are a squash player, try racquetball.
If the alternative sport fails to please, try one of the less closely related sports.

Chapter 4

A Guide to Grips

Starting the Correct Way

How you hold your racquet can have a large bearing on how you play your game, because your grip will often determine how you stroke. Unfortunately or otherwise, each of our major racquet sports has different racquets and different grips. Thus you cannot simply move from one sport to another and use the same grips for each sport in the same way. This chapter will describe how the grips are used for each sport and show you their relative importance.

When you start a new racquet sport or when you switch from one to another, you should either check your grips yourself or have someone watch you play to make sure that you are holding the racquet correctly. Many of the stroking problems of the beginner and even the advanced player can be traced directly to an incorrect grip. Developing the proper grip will help you hit better strokes.

Over the years there have been many styles of gripping the racquet in each sport and just as many theories for each grip. However, many of those theories were simply to support a top player whose abilities allowed him to overcome the deficiencies of a grip that would be very awkward for the weekend sportsman. For example, Bjorn Borg favors an extreme tennis grip, often called a Western grip since it used to be favored by players from the West. Borg's unusual grip helps him add excessive topspin to all his shots, a major feature of his play. However, an ordinary player using such a grip would be lucky to hit the ball at all, much less add topspin to his shots. Borg's timing and racquet control permit him to use the racquet in ways that are not easy for the layman to copy.

The Tennis Grips

Although there are three main types of tennis grip—the Eastern, the Western and the continental—the average racquet sports player would be well advised to stick to one grip, the Eastern, in both its forehand and backhand variations. The Eastern grip is easy to learn, feels comfortable and will prove reliable in most tennis playing situations. We will mention the other two types of grip, but we do not advocate them for the average player.

The Eastern forehand grip (Figure 11) is often called the "shake-hands" grip, since the simplest way of taking up this grip is to shake hands with the racquet. Have someone hold the racquet by the head (strings vertical and the shaft pointing toward you) so you can reach out and grasp the handle as though you were shaking hands. You will naturally wrap your fingers around the handle, and you'll find that your fingers will spread out a little as you close your grip. This is the Eastern forehand. If you'd like to check your grip, make sure that the "V" formed by your thumb and first finger is over the flat of the top of the handle.

This Eastern grip will naturally let you hit your forehands with a slightly laid-back wrist and a racquet face that is close to being vertical. That will help you meet the ball squarely and so help you get the control you'll need to make the ball go where you want it to.

To get an Eastern backhand grip (Figure 12), start with your

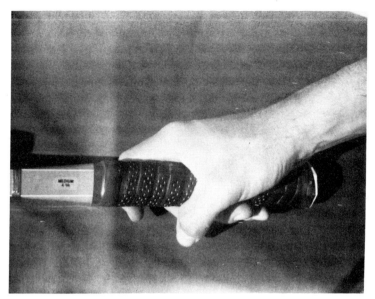

Fig. 11. *Tennis: Eastern forehand grip*

Fig. 12. *Tennis: Eastern backhand grip*

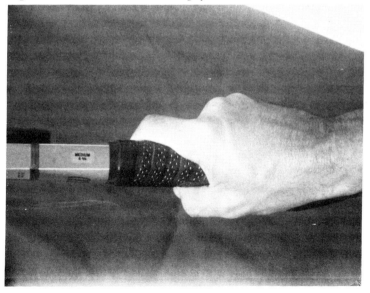

forehand grip and (if you are a right-hander; if not, just reverse these directions) rotate your hand a little less than a quarter of a turn to the left until the ''V'' of your thumb and first finger is over the left bevel of the racquet handle. If you were to hit a forehand with this grip, you would find that the racquet face would be open (that is, facing up slightly), so you would tend to hit balls up in the air unless you could close the racquet face by using your wrist —not an easy thing to do with a backhand grip. However, using your backhand grip on the backhand side will make the racquet face almost vertical as you hit the ball, again helping you to hit the ball firmly and with good control. Your wrist will be behind the racquet so you can put more power into the shot.

With a little practice, you will find these grips are quite instinctive, and you will be able to change from one to the other in play without thinking about them. Initially you may have to use your other hand to make the change, but it is so slight that the racquet can be rotated in one hand without difficulty.

The continental grip (Figure 13) is almost midway between the Eastern forehand and backhand grips. It is a so-called universal grip in that the typical continental player usually does not change grips between the forehand and backhand side. It is often used by players who play on fast surfaces and do not have time to change grips while volleying at the net. In advanced play, there often is very little time to alter a grip in the fast exchanges that take place when playing at the net.

The Western grip (Figure 14), in which the palm of the hand is behind or even below the racquet handle, is little used nowadays except by a few top players who have an excessive topspin game. The Western grip requires very precise racquet head control. It is not suitable for the weekend tennis player unless the player has grown up with the grip and has overcome its innate disadvantages.

So, when you play tennis, you should use the Eastern forehand and backhand grips for your forehand and backhand drives. Initially, you will probably use the same grips for volleying at the net, switching to hit off either side. However, as your game im-

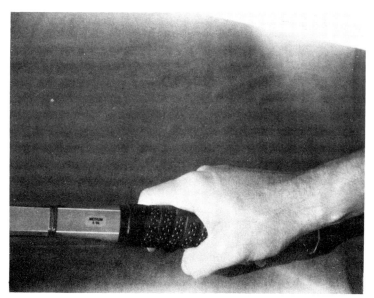

Fig. 13. *Tennis: continental grip*

Fig. 14. *Tennis: Western forehand grip*

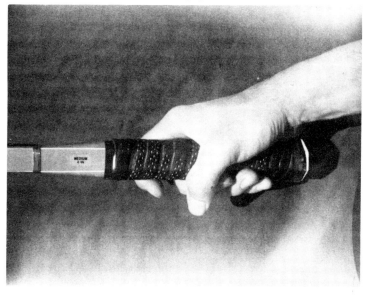

proves you should try to use one grip at the net—probably something close to a continental grip. You will find that it is possible to hit quite an effective forehand volley with a continental grip but much more difficult to hit a backhand volley with a forehand grip.

For the serve, you should try to use a continental grip, although a forehand grip may be easiest at first. To a non-tennis player, that may sound strange, since the serve is hit on the forehand side of the body. However, the serve will not be hit flat, as would be the case if you were to use a forehand grip. A continental grip will let the racquet head brush around the ball as you make contact, thus putting sidespin, or slice, on the ball. This will make for a much more effective serve. You will develop a spin serve without having to make a conscious effort to put spin on the ball. A continental grip also allows more wrist snap, which will add power.

Similarly, it is often better to hit your overheads with a continental grip, since it allows more wrist snap for extra power. However, a perfectly adequate overhead can be hit with a forehand grip.

The other shots of tennis, in particular those such as the lob and the drop shot that call for sensitive touch, are often best hit with a backhand grip or continental, irrespective of which side the shot is hit on. The backhand grip will open the racquet face a little more, which you'll need to hit many of these shots on the forehand side.

The Platform Tennis Grips

Most platform tennis players use the same grips that they would for conventional tennis. If you have never played the sport before, you should begin by using the Eastern grips (Figures 15 and 16) for your forehand and backhand drives. However, as your play improves and the pace increases, you will probably find that you have less time to switch grips during the course of a rally.

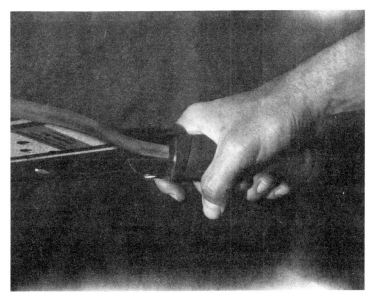

Fig. 15. *Platform tennis: Eastern forehand grip*

Fig. 16. *Platform tennis: Eastern backhand grip*

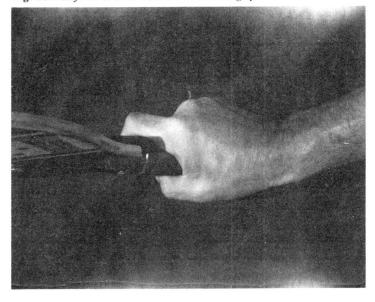

Away from the net, many platform players prefer to use a forehand grip all the time because the forehand is the real workhorse stroke of the sport. If the ball has to be taken on the backhand, it can be hit with a forehand grip because the ball can be lobbed quite easily without changing grips.

At the net, the reverse applies. Although many beginners tend to favor the forehand volley at first, the backhand volley is by far the more flexible shot at the net. Thus it's best to use an Eastern backhand or continental grip at the net and to hit mostly backhand volleys. Because the paddle is so short, backhand volleys can be hit from a wide range of positions, thus reducing the need for a forehand volley and the consequent changing of grip. The court is so narrow that the backhand volley can cover most of your half of the court.

As in tennis, the platform tennis serve is often hit with spin, so a continental grip (Figure 17) is preferable when serving. A beginner may wish to start serving with a forehand grip, but it's preferable to make the change as soon as you have sufficient confidence. Power and spin aren't too important for the platform tennis overhead, so it's best to use a continental grip to hit your overheads, since that's the grip you'll be holding at net most of the time.

The Squash Grip

Squash is unusual among all the major racquet sports in that only one grip is required. Because squash has some very wristy strokes and you must get under low balls, a continental type of grip (Figure 18) is preferred by most players. The continental grip allows wristier shots in any racquet sport and so is particularly suited to squash. In addition, good squash players hold the racquet relatively loosely in the fingers so that extra wrist and finger snap can be added to the shot. The continental grip is most natural when the racquet is held in the fingers rather than in both the fingers and palm as in tennis.

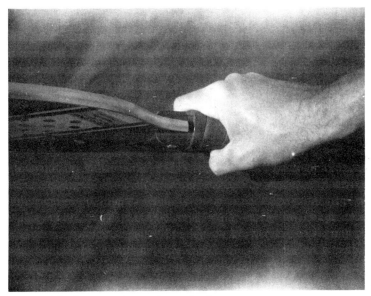

Fig. 17. *Platform tennis: continental grip*

Fig. 18. *Squash: continental grip*

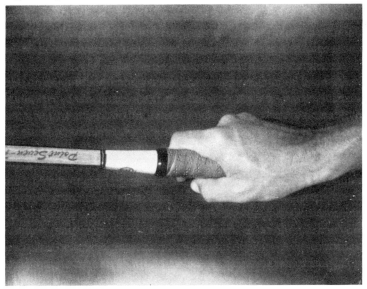

So for squash play there is no change from the forehand to backhand side in terms of altering grips. Drives, volleys and the serve can be hit with the same grip. Attacking and defensive shots are hit with the same grip in the fast-paced play.

Most strokes in squash are hit flat or with very slight underspin or sidespin. Topspin strokes are not used, so the Eastern forehand and backhand grips would offer no advantage to the squash player. Thus a tennis or platform tennis player coming into squash will have to modify his grips and make a distinct effort not to change as the ball comes to one side or the other.

If you have difficulty adapting to the squash grip, think of gripping the racquet as you might a small hammer. The same wristy motion you would use to drive in a nail is the one you will need to achieve in squash, so grip the handle of the racquet as if you were about to perform a precise piece of nailing. But remember that most of the grip must be in your fingers so that you retain the flexibility of your wrist.

The Racquetball Grips

There are a variety of grips used in racquetball, but the newcomer to the sport will be better off using the Eastern forehand and backhand grips (Figures 19 and 20). However, like squash, racquetball is a wristy game, so the racquet should be held more in the fingers than for tennis. In fact, racquetball racquet handles, like squash racquet handles, are generally smaller than their tennis counterparts, so it is easier to hold the racquetball in the fingers for that extra snap.

Many racquetballers favor the Eastern forehand grip most of the time, since the forehand is the most frequently used stroke. The forehand is used for drives, serves and volleys, unlike tennis where the continental grip is generally recommended for the volley and the serve. Attacking shots are hit down with a slightly closed face, which is easier with the forehand grip.

Racquetball's equivalent of the overhead, the ceiling ball, can

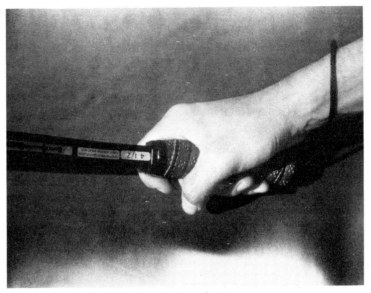

Fig. 19. *Racquetball: Eastern forehand grip*

Fig. 20. *Racquetball: Eastern backhand grip*

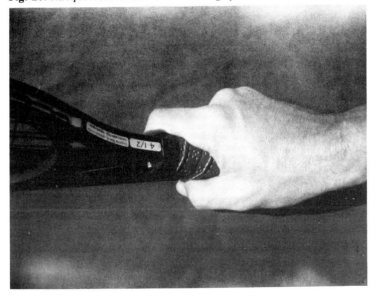

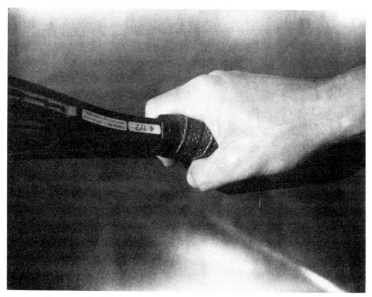

Fig. 21. *Racquetball: continental grip*

be hit off both sides with a proper grip change but is more usually
hit on the forehand side with a forehand grip, since it is a flat shot
without spin. However, you may find that you can hit a wristier
ceiling ball with a grip that tends to the continental (Figure 21),
similar to the squash grip. For an effective ceiling ball, accuracy
is more important than speed, so a strong wrist snap is not essential.

The Badminton Grips

Badminton has two radically different grips—a continental
type (Figure 22) that is used for most strokes and a frying-pan or
panhandle grip (Figure 23) that is used only when playing close
to the net. Some badminton players do switch grips between the
forehand and backhand sides, but the pace of play in competitive
badminton is such that there is little time to think about and make
a significant grip change except for putting the thumb up the back

66

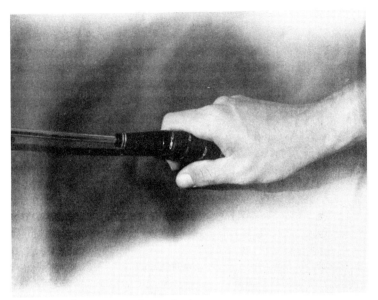

Fig. 22. *Badminton: continental grip*

Fig. 23. *Badminton: frying-pan grip*

on the backhand strokes. Also, like squash and racquetball, badminton is a very wristy game, so the racquet should be held in the fingers, which is easier to do with a continental type of grip.

The frying-pan grip is exactly as its name suggests—it is the grip you would use if you were holding a frying pan over a hot stove. It is similar to the tennis player's Western grip. This grip is used with the racquet held up in front of the player ready to charge the serve or hit sharp volleys at the net, which, of course, is considerably higher than a tennis or platform tennis net. Naturally, shots to either side are handled with this same grip and are hit with the same face of the racquet—unlike, say, volleys in tennis.

The continental grip, used for the other badminton strokes, also permits the use of the wrist—vital in badminton for both power and disguise. Some players modify their grips by putting the thumb up the handle on the backhand for a little extra push. If this helps your shot, there is no reason not to use it. The racquet should be held more in the fingers than in the palm for that extra wrist snap as contact is made with the shuttle. However, do not hold the racquet too far up in the fingers or it may be too loose and could twist as you make contact with the shuttlecock.

When you begin badminton play, particularly if you are a tennis player, you may wish to change grips for forehands and backhands. This will work for you as beginner, but you will soon find that the pace of play is too fast for a full grip change. In effect, you will be forced to adopt a continental type of grip for most of your shots.

Chapter 5

Putting the Ball in Play

The Serve: The Most Critical Racquet Sport Stroke

The serve is, without any doubt, the most critical stroke in each of the racquet sports. Usually, the server has an advantage and is expected to make use of that advantage to win the point. Thus a poor serve will often lose matches while a good server can expect to win frequently. It's not quite that simple, of course, as we will see as we look at other aspects of each of the racquet sports.

Interestingly enough, the serves differ considerably among the five major racquet sports. In fact, the differences are perhaps greater than those of other comparable strokes. So the ability to serve well at, say, squash does not mean you will develop a good tennis serve, too. Thus, if you wish to play several racquet sports, it is in your serve that you will have to make the most significant adjustments. Fortunately, the serves are not all as difficult as the overhead tennis service.

The most important common factor all the racquet sports serves share is that the server is in complete command when serving. The server decides exactly where he wishes to put the ball and where he will go after completing his stroke. The server chooses his position and time of serving. The pressure is almost entirely on the receiver, who has to guess what the server is about to do. It is precisely this element that gives the server his advantage. In all the racquet sports, the server should learn how to exploit this advantage.

Because the server usually holds an edge, players determine who serves first by spinning a racquet or tossing a coin. The winner of the toss normally serves first, except in tennis or platform tennis, where a player who is a slow starter may decide to receive first. The server expects to win the first game or points and so start out, at least psychologically, ahead of his opponent, who then has to catch up. Similarly, a player who loses his first serve will often boost the confidence of his opponent. Thus, psychology plays an important part in serving.

Curiously, despite the importance of the serve, few racquet sports players devote the time to practicing their serves that they should. The serve is the one stroke that can always be practiced without a partner and, if necessary, in complete isolation. So when you move from one racquet sport to another, we suggest that you spend considerable time working on your serve. You can also experiment with your serves without having to consider your practice partner. Few racquet sports players experiment sufficiently.

Now let's take a look at the various serves, starting with the simplest, although not necessarily the easiest, the badminton serve, and progressing through racquetball and squash to tennis and platform tennis.

The Badminton Serve: A Defensive Action

The badminton serve looks relatively simple—the player drops the shuttlecock from about shoulder height and then hits it from below the waist (with the racquet head lower than the wrist), using an underarm racquet motion. Thus the beginning player will find the serve quite easy to pick up and will hit a legal serve without much difficulty. The problems arise in trying to hit a serve that cannot easily be attacked by the receiver. Thus a badminton serve tends to be a defensive action because the server hits up and aims for a limited court space.

In singles play, one player serves until he loses a point, whereupon the serve passes to his opponent. The serving court is determined by the score—if the server's score is an even number, the player serves from the right-hand court, if odd, from the left. Doubles play is somewhat more complicated (see rules in Appendix). The server must stand with both feet behind the short service line (see Figure 7) in the correct half of the court, and the shuttlecock must be hit so that, if not returned by the receiver, it would fall within the opposite service court.

There is one other important distinction in the badminton serve: a let (where the shuttlecock touches the net) is considered to be still in play, although most let serves will probably fall short of the service court. However, you should always be ready to play a let serve.

Only the server may score, so when the receiver makes an error the server gains a point. If the server hits a fault, the receiver gains only the opportunity to serve. Thus, it is possible for one side to have a long scoring streak or conversely, for many points to take place without any addition to the score.

There are four badminton serves (Figure 24)—the short serve, the flick, the drive and the high serve. The two most frequently used are the short serve, hit low over the net to drop rapidly in the front of the opponent's service court, and the high serve, hit high and deep to the back of the opposing service court. Because the doubles service court is shorter, the high serve is much less used in doubles. In singles, both serves are used but the high serve is often favored since it pulls the opponent away from the net and is not easily attacked. The flick and drive serves are very similar. The flick serve is a quick serve intended to just clear the receiver's racquet while the drive is a quick serve hit almost directly at the receiver.

Most badminton players serve off the forehand side. The high

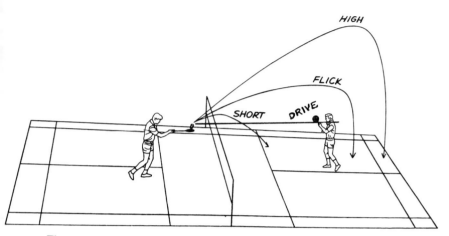

Fig. 24. *The badminton serves (short, flick, and high)*

serve is an underarm swing starting with the racquet high and the wrist cocked. The server hits the shuttlecock in front of his body using a pronounced wrist snap at impact. There is an extended follow-through. On the short serve (Figure 25), the player follows through to about shoulder height, whereas on the high serve the racquet action is faster and the follow-through more extended.

On the short serve, the shuttlecock should reach its highest point before crossing the net but should not fall so rapidly that it will not cross the short service line. If the shuttle is still rising as it crosses the net, the receiver will be able to hit down on it aggressively and, most likely, win the point. Thus, touch and careful placement are absolutely vital on the short serve so that it is not easily attacked.

For a high serve, the wrist should be uncocked sharply on contact so the shuttlecock will go high in the air before slowing and dropping deep in the other court. This serve must have enough forward motion to take the shuttlecock deep and sufficient upward motion to take it over the receiver's outstretched racquet on the way up. It is harder for the novice to develop an accurate high serve than a competent short serve.

72

Fig. 25. *The badminton serving stroke*

With both serves, disguise is important. Since a badminton serve is very dependent, as are almost all badminton shots, on wrist action, the shot can be carefully disguised right up to the moment of impact. An opponent can be deceived as to not only the type of serve but also its direction. Proper use of disguise will help the server prevent the receiver from getting set to make an attacking return.

One final point; in badminton, server and receiver face each other and are only a few feet apart, so there is often a certain amount of face-to-face psychology involved in serving. One of the greater pleasures of the game is in fooling the receiver and so winning the serve.

The Racquetball Serve: An Attacking Shot

Like the first service in tennis, the racquetball first serve is an attacking shot where the player tries to win the point outright or set up a weak return. The server has a distinct advantage and

73

usually makes the most of it. In fact, play at the professional level can be dominated by a stronger server who consistently wins his serves. However, at the amateur level a good server does not possess quite the same towering advantage over the receiver.

To serve, a racquetballer stands within the service zone (see Figure 10), bounces the ball on the floor and hits it with an underarm action against the front wall so that it rebounds, sometimes touching one of the sidewalls, to bounce on the floor beyond the short line. An improper serve may be a "fault" or an "out." If the player hits a fault serve, he can serve a second time. Two faults and the serve passes to his opponent. If the player hits an out serve, his opponent becomes the server.

There are several ways of hitting a fault serve (see rules in Appendix), but the most frequent are hitting a ball that falls in front of the short line, a ball that hits both sidewalls before bouncing on the floor or a ball that hits either the ceiling or the back wall before touching the floor. The more serious error—that of hitting an out serve—occurs when the server misses the ball or touches it with his body, or the ball hits the ceiling, sidewall or floor before hitting the front wall.

Since only the server can score points and he continues to serve as long as he wins the point, it's vital for the racquetballer to hold serve, and the ability to serve well is an important part of the game. Although the racquetball serving action is essentially simple, a player must put a lot of variety into his serve in order to stay on top of the match.

Unlike most other racquet sports, there are no left and right service courts in racquetball, so the server may stand anywhere he chooses in the service zone and may serve off either hand into either side of the court. However, most servers use their forehand swing for serving, since that is usually a player's most powerful and reliable shot, and most serves are aimed to the receiver's backhand (the left side of the court for a right-handed receiver).

There are three principal racquetball serves (Figure 26): the soft or "garbage" serve; the hard or "drive" serve; and the "Z"

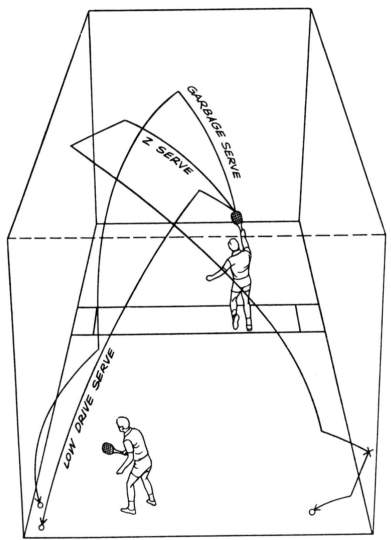

Fig. 26. *The racquetball serves (drive, garbage and Z serves)*

serve, which hits the front wall, then a sidewall, crosses the court bouncing on the floor and finally hits the opposite sidewall on a Z-shaped path. There are several variations on each of these serves but the basic principles are much the same—to keep the receiver deep in the backcourt while the server protects the center court position, from which most attacking shots can be made and reached.

The most common racquetball serve, especially with novices, is the garbage serve. The player stands in the middle of the service zone, hits the ball relatively gently so that it hits the front wall about halfway up and closer to the sidewall (the left sidewall when facing a right-handed receiver). The ball rebounds high off the front wall, bouncing just behind the short line and then, preferably, dies in the back corner. A good garbage serve usually forces a defensive return, such as a ceiling ball (see Chapter 6). The garbage serve is hit with a lifting or lobbing motion so the ball bounces upward off the front wall. The garbage serve has a fairly easy action that most beginners can handle without much practice. Unfortunately, if hit badly, the ball may bounce off the sidewall into the center of the court where it will become an easy setup for the receiver. So the garbage serve requires careful placement and touch.

The drive serve is, as its name suggests, struck hard and relatively low against the front wall so that it rebounds to hit the floor just past the short line. To hit a drive serve, the ball is bounced low and the server uses a powerful swing so that contact is made below knee level (Figure 27). A normal forehand stroke is used with the pronounced wrist snap characteristic of racquetball drives. A drive serve must be hit hard and accurately, so the receiver has to stay well back to return the ball. A poor drive will let the receiver move up and attempt a winning shot.

Although it looks complicated, the Z serve is relatively easy to hit. It offers the advantage of being confusing for the receiver, who may be unable to decide when to hit the ball or to judge the rebounds accurately. The Z serve must be hit quite hard, since it must rebound from three walls and has to travel a considerable

Fig. 27. *The racquetball drive serving stroke*

distance. The Z serve should be hit from one side of the service zone to contact the front wall about halfway up near the opposite corner. The ball will then rebound from the sidewall and cross the court. It must bounce on the floor before hitting the opposite sidewall to be a legal serve.

The server has to be careful that he does not get in the way of the ball as it ricochets across the court and must give the ball enough speed to travel all the way across. A short Z serve will go to the receiver's forehand for an easy return. A good Z serve will be spinning violently as it comes off the sidewall, which will make for a difficult return.

Although a beginner will often use the garbage serve for both first and second serves and it can be effective at any level of play, the drive serve is favored by more advanced players. A powerful drive serve may ace the opponent or force an error, whereas a garbage serve can be returned easily and may start a long ceiling ball rally (see Chapter 6).

When you begin racquetball play, you should aim for depth on your serves. Serves that bounce midway between the short line and the backwall will usually die close to the back wall or the corner, where they are hardest to return. Aim most of your serves at your opponent's backhand, since that is usually everyone's weakness. However, an occasional serve to the forehand side will keep the receiver guessing.

Disguise is not as important in racquetball as in badminton, although the receiver waits behind the server where it's hardest to figure out what he's going to do. Variation is the key, in both speed and placement. A wide variety in serves can compensate for a lack of power.

The Squash Serve: Taking the Offensive

The squash serve is usually a finesse shot, but without the vulnerability of the badminton serve. While it is perfectly possible for a good server to win the point outright off a serve, fewer points are won that way than in racquetball. This is mainly due to the smaller court and deader ball—a hard-hit squash serve, if not placed correctly, will come off the back wall where the receiver can make an easy return. Thus, the hard squash serve calls for control more than power. As we noted earlier, this is a distinguishing characteristic between racquetball and squash—the latter demands more in terms of racquet and ball control.

To serve, the player stands with one foot inside the appropriate service box (and not touching any of the lines—that would be a foot fault). The ball may be thrown in the air or bounced on the floor. The player then strokes the ball so it hits the front wall above the service line but below the out-of-play line and rebounds so, if left to fall, it bounces on the floor within the opposite service court. If the serve is a fault, the player may serve again from the same service box. If he double-faults, he loses the point and the serve passes to his opponent, who can then choose which box he wishes to serve from. If the server wins the point, he takes his next serve from the other service box, and so on. He continues to serve until he loses a point.

In the international game, only the server can score points but the principles of serving are much the same. In both the American and international games, a player should attempt to hold his serve for as long as possible. When serving, the player is in an offensive position where, all else being equal, he should expect to win the point. After serving, he will be closest to the midcourt position (the "T" formed by the service courts and the service line) where he can ordinarily expect to control the point. We'll have more to say about the importance of the T later.

A serve is obviously a fault if it does not hit the front wall correctly or fails to bounce within the opposite service court. However, the server will also fault if he misses the ball or if his foot touches the lines of the service box. He will fault if the ball touches a sidewall or the floor before hitting the front wall or if the ball touches the ceiling or any wall beyond the out-of-play lines at any stage in its flight. However, unlike tennis, the lines marking a squash court are not "good." A ball must hit or bounce *inside* the lines to be considered good.

There are two significant varieties of squash serve—the hard and soft serves (Figure 28). As in racquetball, there are a number of variations of each type of serve, and a good server will use as much variety as possible in serving to keep the receiver guessing and to stop him from moving in anticipation of the serve. The objective of the server is to keep the receiver back deep in the court so the server can stay up in the important T position. Thus, placement of the serve is much more critical than the power of the server. A player who can consistently place his serve well

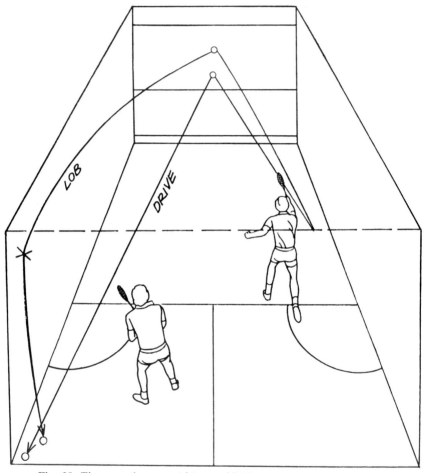

Fig. 28. *The squash serves (drive and lob)*

will win more points than the power server who tends to be erratic. This is especially true when playing with the bouncy 70+ ball.

The slow, or lob, serve is the safest and, consequently, the most frequently used squash serve. The slow serve not only is relatively easy to hit but also gives the server more time to get into the T position where he can stay on top of the play. The slow serve is hit with an underhand action so that the ball strikes the front wall high and a little to the left of center (if serving from the right service box), rebounding down to touch the sidewall close to the backwall before dropping to bounce on the floor near the backwall. A good lob serve will not come off the backwall before bouncing on the floor.

Since the ideal lob serve should almost "kiss" the sidewall, this serve is hit to an opponent's backhand when serving from the right service box and to his forehand when serving from the left box. Most receivers will attempt to volley the serve before it bounces, so the closer the ball hugs the sidewall the better. A ball that flies close to the wall will be difficult to hit without the receiver striking the wall with his racquet.

The slow serve is hit with a half stroke, starting with the racquet relatively low and the wrist cocked back (Figure 29). The server lets go of the ball as the racquet comes forward so as to make contact at waist height or lower. The wrist is snapped forward as the ball is hit but very little spin is applied to the ball. The follow-through is high across the player's body. Weight transfer is not critical for this shot, but a full follow-through will help the server maintain control of the ball and so get the correct placement that is essential for the slow serve.

The hard service uses a very different arm action from that of the slow serve. It is hit with an overarm swing somewhat like the action of a baseball pitcher. Although it is a powerful shot, the hard service does not use the full roundhouse swing of the tennis serve but does use a very pronounced wrist snap to get the racquet head moving as quickly as possible at impact with the ball.

The ball is tossed in the air, just in front of the forward shoulder

Fig. 29. *The squash lob serving stroke*

(the left shoulder for a right-handed player). The racquet is taken up and back quickly with a sharply cocked wrist so that the racquet head almost touches the opposite shoulder. The racquet is then swung forward with a pitching action so the racquet head meets the ball a little above and to the right of the player, and the follow-through is across the body. Since some body weight is thrown into this shot, it's important to keep your balance throughout, but be ready to move rapidly to the T or out of the line of fire after completing the stroke.

The hard serve should strike the front wall as low as possible but may rebound either straight at the opponent or deep in the opposite corner. A good hard serve will hit the back wall low before dropping to the floor. If it bounces before hitting the back wall, the ball will stand up and give the receiver a chance to make an easy return. However, a receiver will often attempt to volley a hard serve before it reaches the back wall, so the lower the serve, the harder it will be to return. As with the lob serve, placement is critical—a badly placed hard serve not only will be easy to return but will cause the server to lose the T position.

The Tennis Serve: The Big Weapon

The serve is without doubt the key stroke of tennis. It is an enormous advantage to be the server in tennis, so the strong server will rarely lose to opponents of similar general ability. Because the rules of tennis permit the server two attempts at getting the ball in play, the first serve is generally a powerful shot that may win the point outright—an "ace" in tennis terms—or will force a weak return from the receiver. Even if the server faults on his first serve, he has the benefit of a second try—an insurance policy. Although double faults are by no means uncommon, a second serve should miss only rarely.

Ordinarily, the server should expect to win each of the games in which he serves (or his doubles team serves)—in other words, to "hold" his serve. If his opponent fails to win one of his service games, his serve is said to be "broken." The terminology is apt, since a server who fails to hold serve will usually lose the set, whereas the server who breaks his opponent's serve will win the set. A set of tennis can be won with only one break of serve and it is possible to win a match with only two breaks of serve (unless tie-breakers are used). Thus the server should always hold his serve.

To serve, the server stands behind the baseline, between the center mark and the sideline, throws the ball in the air and hits it so that it crosses the net and bounces in the opposite service court. If the serve is a fault, the server will serve again from the same general position. The first serve of a game is always from the right-hand court into the opponent's right service court (often called the "deuce" court because the deuce, or 40-40, point will always be served into that court). The serve alternates to each service court as the points are played.

A serve will be a fault if it fails to bounce in the correct service court. A serve is also a fault if the server misses the ball completely, if it bounces before crossing the net, if it does not cross the net or if it hits a post before bouncing in the proper court. The server commits a foot fault if his feet touch any part of the baseline before or during contact with the ball. If the ball touches the top of the net but otherwise bounces in the proper court, the serve is a "let" and must be replayed.

There are three basic types of serve—the flat, the slice and the twist (Figure 30). Most novices use a flat serve, in which the ball is hit with the racquet strings perpendicular to the ball's direction. Such a serve has little or no spin and travels in a straight line (allowing for the usual effects of gravity, of course). The flat serve is also used by advanced players when they wish to hit a very high-speed serve, the cannonball serve, in the hopes of scoring an ace. So the flat serve can be used at any level of the game, but the beginner should go for consistency rather than aces.

The slice serve requires a little more skill in hitting the ball and getting the desired direction. The ball is hit with the racquet head moving sideways slightly during contact so that spin is put on the ball. The spin makes the ball drop, which helps it to fall more reliably into the proper service court. More importantly, the ball will curve sideways through the air, either toward or away from the receiver, making for a more difficult return. Thus, the slice serve is generally a feature of the improving player's game. It is used as either a first or second serve but is especially useful as a second, because the spin helps the ball drop into the service box and so gives a greater margin for error.

By contrast, the twist or "kick" serve is much more difficult to execute but also can be much tougher for the receiver to return adequately. A correctly hit twist serve will have mostly topspin, which makes the serve kick high in the air after bouncing in the service court. A ball that bounces so high will often result in a

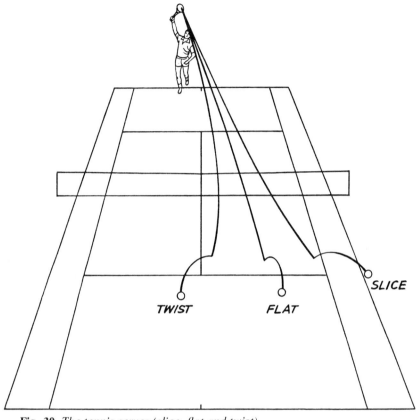

Fig. 30. *The tennis serves (slice, flat and twist)*

return that is very weak. Generally, only more advanced players have sufficient skill to hit a twist serve properly. A badly hit twist can produce a weak serve that can be devoured by the receiver. The twist is often used as a second serve by more advanced players.

All three serves are hit with a similar overhead motion (Figure 31). The ball is tossed in the air, the racquet taken back behind the shoulders and then swung forward to hit the ball with maximum extension of the body and arm. The swing is as full as

85

Fig. 31. *The tennis serving stroke*

possible and the server follows through until the racquet ends up
pointing behind him. As much weight as possible is transferred
forward as the server goes through the stroke. This weight transfer will add extra power to the shot. The wrist is often cocked
before contact so that it may be snapped through the impact with
the ball. The serve and the overhead smash are the only tennis
strokes that consistently use wrist snap.

It is perfectly legal to hit a tennis serve with an underhand motion, but such a serve will often be weak and therefore easily returned by the opponent. However, a player with back or shoulder injuries might find the underhand serve an acceptable substitute until the injuries heal.

Perhaps more so than in the other racquet sports, the tennis serve requires a great deal of timing and coordination. Most beginners have trouble timing their serves, and even better players will experience days when their timing is so bad that their serves suffer badly. Not only does the ball have to be placed correctly in the air, so that it is almost motionless at the top of its flight just before contact, but for an effective serve the whole motion of the arm and racquet should be smooth and without any pause or hitch. With the added need for body weight transfer, putting the several elements of the serve together at the right time and place can be infuriatingly difficult for the newcomer to the sport.

However, the serve is a singularly attractive stroke to both the player and the spectator. The player will know instinctively that he has got it right when the serve seems almost effortlessly smooth and powerful. The best servers among the professional players, such as Arthur Ashe and John Newcombe, have service motions that look relaxed and simple. And, incidentally, the example of Ashe shows that you do not have to be a big player to have a formidable serve. Timing is the key to a good serve—not strength.

The ability to hit an effective serve is only half the battle in tennis. You must also be able to place the serve exactly where you wish. We do not have space to go into all the strategic aspects of serving, but we can indicate a few basic ideas.

You will quickly realize that tennis is a game in which you should play to your opponent's weakness. Nowhere is this more true than with the serve. With ordinary players, the backhand is generally the weakest shot for returning serve, so hit most of your serves deep to your opponent's backhand. However, don't continually go for the backhand or a smart player will recognize your tactic and begin to move over so that he can take more of your serves on his stronger forehand. You can keep your opponent honest by mixing up your serves.

In the deuce court, you will generally be better off keeping most of your serves down the middle of the court so that your opponent cannot return with a sharp angle. However, if you slice your serves, you may want to serve wide into the deuce court (assuming that you are right-handed), so that the curve of the ball's flight will pull the receiver wide and so may give you a service ace, or winner. In fact, when you can slice your serve, you should experiment with different placements to see which ones give your opponent the most trouble. Some players, for example, have great difficulty with a serve that curves in toward them, such as a slice down the middle into the deuce court.

There are significant differences in serving to a right- and a left-handed player. For the lefties, remember that everything is reversed. A righty's backhand side is a lefty's forehand, so simply switch the direction of the majority of your serves.

As you can see, the possibilities for strategic variations of the serve are endless. You will have to find the variations that work best for you. Even world-class players never cease to work on their serves. The serve is such an important part of tennis that no one can afford to neglect it, and there is no player who does not need improvement. There is only one way to a better serve and that is to practice and experiment. Unfortunately, many tennis players seem unwilling to make the investment in time and effort that a good serve requires. But in tennis there is no substitute for a good serve: it is the key stroke of the sport.

The Platform Tennis Serve: Only One Chance

The rules of serving in platform tennis are much the same as for regular tennis, with one significant exception—only one serve is permitted. This makes the serve a very different shot in platform tennis. A player no longer has the luxury of a big first serve, secure in the knowledge that he can always depend on getting his second serve in. And the receiver can put enormous pressure on the server in the hope of causing him to hit a fault. Thus, there is a strong psychological aspect to the platform tennis serve.

Given the reduced dimensions of a platform tennis court, serving is comparatively easy. In fact, too much power is a real disadvantage in platform play, since a ball that is hit too hard will rebound off the wires so the receiver can make an easy return. Thus, the ace serve of tennis is almost impossible in platform tennis.

As in tennis, serves may be hit overhead or underhand, but the latter style is almost never used. The motion of serving (Figure 32) is more compact than for a tennis serve. The player tosses the

Fig. 32. *The platform tennis serving stroke*

ball out in front so he will have to lean into the serve, takes the racquet back behind his head (the roundhouse preparatory swing and deep backscratching position of tennis are not necessary for platform), and swings smartly forward with a wrist snap at contact, completing the stroke with a full follow-through.

Most beginners use a forehand grip to serve, resulting in a flat shot, which is quite adequate for novice play. However, better players, as in tennis, will favor a grip that is more toward the continental, so that sidespin can be applied to the serve. The newer fiberglass and aluminum paddles often have a rough surface, which aids spin production, thus encouraging the use of a continental grip for the serve.

No matter what the level of play, a platform tennis server will always follow his serve to the net, so the server will transfer his weight forward as he makes contact with the ball, stepping into the court and continuing on up to the service line to volley back the opponent's return.

As in tennis, the real key to the platform tennis serve is to get the ball in deep (Figure 33). Since only one serve is permitted, beginners often have a tendency to almost drop their serves into the service box. This is a mistake, since the receiver will come in to take the serve early and, most likely, hit a blistering return right at the feet of the oncoming server. The server will then have a tough time digging the ball out from down by his feet. So the serve must be hit deep but not so hard that the ball will readily bounce off the wires if it goes past the receiver. A good serve will keep the receiver back so that he cannot hit an easy return, or if he chooses to let the ball come off the screens, the ball will almost die or spin erratically off the wires.

When the receiver realizes that his opponent does not serve well, he will move in to attempt to intimidate the server. Such psychology is an essential part of platform play. So it is very important that a platform player have a dependable serve that will go in at least 90 percent of the time. That is why the better players often favor a spin serve. The spin helps bring the ball down into the court, so providing a greater margin of error for the

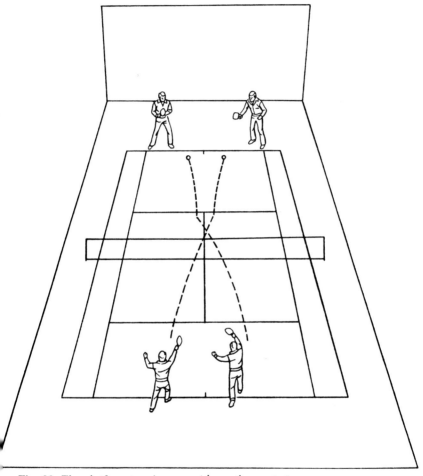

Fig. 33. *The platform tennis serves (down the center)*

server. The spin will also make the ball curve through the air both before and after the bounce, making for a more difficult return.

In platform play, the serving team usually holds the advantage over the opponents, but that edge cannot be maintained without a good serve. So although the serve is not as powerful a weapon as in some of the other racquet sports, it is just as critical a stroke. A newcomer to the sport should spend some time on practicing his serve, striving to get the depth and placement that will help him keep the advantage when serving.

Chapter 6

How to Hit the Longer Strokes

The Basic Strokes

In each of our five major racquet sports, there are certain basic strokes you will need to start with. Although these strokes have similar names, they are by no means identical in terms of stroking mechanics or use. However, they can all be grouped together so that you can see the relationships among them.

We have rather arbitrarily divided the strokes of the sports into two categories (with the exception of the serve, which was discussed in the last chapter), which are the *longer strokes* (those requiring a full swing) and the *shorter strokes* (those generally requiring only an abbreviated stroke). While this division cannot be exact for each of the sports and, no doubt, will not please the purists in each of the five sports, we think this simplifies things for the nonexpert racquet sports player.

Thus, this chapter will be concerned mainly with the longer strokes—the forehand and backhand drives, the overhead and the lob-like strokes—for each of our sports. The next chapter will look at the shorter strokes such as the volleys and other touch shots. We'll examine each of the major strokes for the sports mainly to pick out the similarities and differences. We will not attempt to show you in detail how to hit each of these strokes, but since we assume that you play at least one of our major sports, we hope we'll be giving you enough information to see how the strokes are performed in the other sports.

The Forehand

We begin with the forehand because that is the stroke that most people will use first no matter what the racquet sport. The forehand seems a natural stroke to most players because that is the way they have been used to hitting objects, whether a ball or some other childhood device. The forehand is important because, with the exception of badminton, it is usually the dominant stroke at the novice and intermediate levels of our sports.

In tennis, the forehand is without question a dominant stroke, to such a degree that many players will run around a ball on the backhand side in order to hit it with the easier forehand. At the higher levels of the game, running around is often not possible due to the speed of the play—and, of course, more advanced players will always have an effective backhand.

The essential characteristics of the tennis forehand are a very big backswing, a forward swing with body movement to put weight into the shot, ball contact with a locked wrist and an extensive follow-through. These characteristics are necessary because the tennis ball is relatively heavy and has to travel the full length of the court (more than 90 feet for a crosscourt shot).

Although beginners usually hit the ball flat, better tennis players often hit their forehands with some topspin. The topspin allows the ball to be hit high over the net for depth but will also pull the ball down into the opponent's court so it does not go too long. Topspin (Figure 34) is quite easily generated with a forward swing that starts low—below the flight of the oncoming ball—and continues up through contact and into the follow-through.

For pace and power, the tennis forehand is best hit with a considerable amount of body motion, somewhat like the baseball batter going after a home run. The body must be turned sideways to the ball's flight, and the player must transfer his weight forward as he hits the ball to add extra power to the shot. Although beginners can get the ball over the net by swinging from the shoulder, pace and depth are much more easily achieved when the player steps into the stroke. This contrasts with the other racquet sports, where weight transfer is less important and much of the pace of a shot comes from the use of excessive wrist snap. Tennis forehands, of course, are hit with no wrist snap, since such shots would often lack control.

The platform tennis forehand (Figure 35) is very similar to the tennis stroke in that it plays a dominant part in the game and is usually hit with a locked wrist. Even more than in tennis, platform players run around their backhands in order to hit forehands. Returns of serve, for example, are almost always hit on the forehand side.

Fig. 34. *The effect of topspin on a tennis ball*

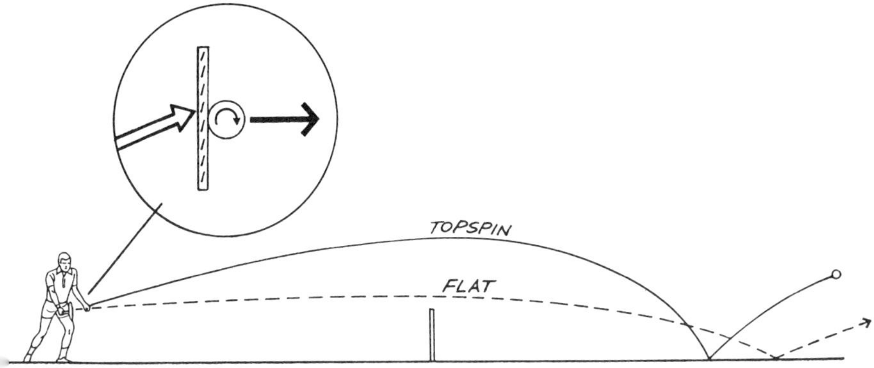

Fig. 35. *The platform tennis forehand*

However, there are some important differences between the two sports. Since the platform court is half the length of a tennis court, rather less power is needed in hitting the ball. Consequently, the forehand backswing is more compact in platform play, although contact is still made with a firm wrist and the follow-through is long and sweeping, as in tennis. However, virtually all platform forehands are hit flat or with a little topspin; the dimensions of the court and the construction of the paddle make heavy topspin less effective, so it is not often used.

Platform players can generate enough power in their forehands without putting much body weight into the shot. And often there simply isn't enough time in the fast action of the platform court to get set and hit the ball in the manner of a ground-stroking tennis player. Quickness of the racquet hand is much more important than the ability to transfer weight into the shot, although the best forehand returns of serve always have weight transfer. Tennis players often have difficulty making this adjustment and in hitting with a shorter backswing.

The forehands of squash and racquetball differ markedly from those of tennis and platform tennis, although they are dominant strokes in all four sports. Both squash and racquetball call for very wristy forehands hit with a semicircular swing that almost resembles a golf swing.

In squash, the racquet is taken back high in the air with a pronounced cocking of the wrist and then brought down and forward to meet the ball quite close to the floor. The cocked wrist lets the squash player hit with a whipping action and lots of wrist snap. Although the good squash player will put some weight into his shots, it is this wrist snap that gives the shot much of its power.

Squash forehands are usually hit flat, or with a little underspin or sidespin by a better player. The underspin (Figure 36) will help the ball drop quickly off the front wall, making for a difficult return by the opponent, while sidespin provides deception. Since

Fig. 36. *The effect of underspin on a squash ball*

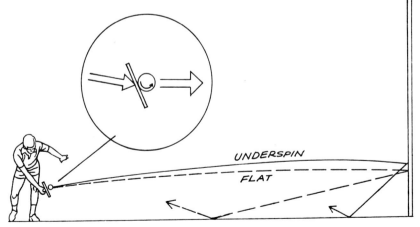

there is no net in a squash court, topspin would not help a squash player. However, underspin or even a little sidespin can be useful for the more advanced player.

Although the squash forehand has a high backswing, the follow-through is usually abbreviated, if only to avoid hitting the opponent or making contact with the wall in the cramped confines of the squash court. Since most of the power is added by the wrist snap, a long follow-through isn't needed to prevent a slowing of the racquet head through contact with the ball. The shorter follow-through also allows the player to recover quickly and get into position to hit his next shot.

In racquetball, the forehand is a very dominant shot. In fact, many intermediate players simply do not possess a backhand drive and will hit ceiling balls or lobs if forced to take the ball on the backhand side. As a result, racquetballers will usually try to run around a backhand to take the ball on their forehand side. Since racquetball at the novice and intermediate levels is a slower-paced game than squash, running around the backhand is quite feasible.

The swing itself is very much like the squash forehand swing, with the racquet taken back high behind the player and the wrist severely cocked. The ball is usually hit at knee height or lower, so the swing again looks like that of a golfer, except that the racquet head is not dropped below the wrist. The ball is hit flat with very little spin, since the objective of the game is to hit the ball hard and low to the front wall. The stroke is similar to the drive serve (see Figure 27). Unlike squash, there is no "tin" on the front wall of a racquetball court, so the ball is aimed as low as possible to the wall, and underspin is not especially useful.

Contact is made with a pronounced wrist snap to impart extra power to the shot. The shorter racquet makes snapping the wrist easier than in squash, so most novice players develop some wrist snap quite naturally. However, the snap has to be exaggerated for a powerful kill shot low to the front wall.

In keeping with the need to generate lots of power, weight transfer and a full follow-through are important for the racquetball forehand drive. The player usually tries to get sideways to the ball and uses a lot of body motion to put weight into the shot. The more weight transfer and wrist snap, the more powerful the shot.

The badminton forehand is also a wristy shot but, due to the nature of the game, is little used except in doubles. Since the badminton court has a high net and the shuttles cannot bounce, most badminton shots are hit with the racquet above the head. The badminton equivalent of a forehand drive is a stroke with a sidearm swing where the racquet is swung on a plane almost parallel with the floor and contact with the bird is made between waist and shoulder height.

The action of the sidearm stroke resembles throwing a ball sidearm. The arm is drawn back and around the body, and the wrist is cocked. The length of the backswing varies with the time available to prepare but usually is quite short.

The dominant shot of badminton is the overhead clear, which we'll look at it in more detail later in this chapter.

The Backhand

In each of our major racquet sports the backhand is the natural complement to the forehand. A well-rounded player will be expected to possess a useful backhand. However, few club players are strong on the backhand side. This may be because the forehand is an easier shot, whereas the backhand often seems awkward to the beginning player. At the higher levels of tennis, at least, the backhand is often a more dependable stroke than the forehand, perhaps because top players spend much more time working on their backhand. Nonetheless, a complete racquet sports player should have a competent backhand in his chosen sports.

As we've noted, in tennis the forehand is by far the stronger shot for the average player. It is a commonplace saying to "attack the backhand" in the often successful hope of forcing an error.

Much of the difficulty that ordinary players experience with the backhand may be due to poor preparation. The backhand requires a proper backswing with a turning of the body. The forward swing should lead into a long follow-through, and the player must transfer his weight into the shot to get sufficient power to hit a ball the length of the court (Figure 37).

The preparation of the average player is often hindered by a habit of waiting for a shot with a forehand grip. Not only is the player physically ready for a forehand, but he is mentally prepared for that stroke. Thus, when the ball comes on the backhand side, both a mental and a physical adjustment have to be made and in very short order.

Most tennis players favor the underspin backhand, since it is easier to take the racquet back high and hit through the ball from high to low. This gives a natural underspin or slicing action. Although underspin shots are not especially safe—they tend to "float," which gives the opponent more time to set up and hit a

Fig. 37. *The tennis backhand*

good return—a player can control the ball on the racquet better and so hit deep or short as the occasion demands. Topspin backhands, while no more difficult mechanically, require more precise timing to hit accurately and, for the club player, can be difficult to control adequately.

The two-handed backhand has become very popular in recent years, due perhaps in no small measure to its use by two top players, Chris Evert and Jimmy Connors. The two-handed shot is excellent for players who have a weak one-handed backhand. The use of the other hand will result in a firmer contact with the ball and so produce a more powerful and controlled shot. Disguise is easier since the ball can be hit later than with the one-handed variety. However, using two hands shortens the reach, so the player must be positioned nearer the ball, which calls for faster footwork and an exaggerated body turn. Therefore a two-handed player must compensate for the shorter reach or use one hand when stretched wide for a backhand.

No matter what type of backhand you prefer, there are two key points to keep in mind. First, the backhand in tennis requires an exceedingly firm wrist—firmer if possible than on the forehand. A very firm wrist will give the precise control that is the hallmark of the good backhand artist, such as Ken Rosewall, whose backhands appear almost effortless but are placed with the precision of a surgeon. Second, you must get into position early and sideways to the flight of the ball so you can transfer your body weight into the shot. Merely strong-arming a backhand will not produce enough power. It is important to step toward the ball and flow into the shot with your weight moving forward at contact with the ball. These two points will go a long way toward removing much of the weakness that many club players have on the backhand side.

In platform tennis, the backhand is a weaker stroke than in tennis. In fact, many platform players have such an inadequate backhand that they will either hit a soft, defensive shot or merely toss up a lob to get out of the particular tight spot that they're in. Much of this backhand weakness is due not so much to neglect as to the speed of platform play. The players simply do not have enough time to get properly set to hit an effective backhand because they are usually set to hit a forehand. As a result, they cannot get much leverage on the ball, and the best backhand that can be produced is often very much weaker than a forehand. Of course, many platform players will run around the backhand to hit a forehand for just the foregoing reasons.

When a backhand is required, the keys to the platform tennis stroke are pretty much the same as for conventional tennis. You must prepare early for the shot and hit the ball with a very firm wrist. If you can't do this, lob or dink (a soft shot hit low over the net). Some players attempt to use a wristy shot on the backhand, but this is tough to do against a hard-hit and heavy ball. Even if there is insufficient time to set up correctly, a firm wrist will help you block the ball back, which will often produce a better return than a poorly executed wristy shot.

As in tennis, many platform players will wait for a shot with a forehand grip, since they expect to take the majority of their balls on that side. If the grip is not changed to hit a backhand, the paddle face will be too open to hit a drive, and so a lob is the more natural result. Thus, you may wish to hit a lob for most of the balls that come to your backhand.

By contrast, the squash backhand is a much more important shot. A good squash player must be able to hit drives off either side, since there often is neither time nor room to run around and hit a forehand. There is very little difference in the manner of stroking a backhand or a forehand. Both shots call for a high backswing, an emphatic body turn to set up for the shot, pronounced wrist snap at contact and a long follow-through (Figure 38). However, the follow-through may be abbreviated when there's a chance of hitting the opponent or even the walls of the court.

The same grip is used for both forehand and backhand (see Chapter 4). Unlike tennis, the grip is not tight except for a moment as the ball is hit. Much of the snap in squash comes from a last-moment tightening of the grip in the fingers as contact is

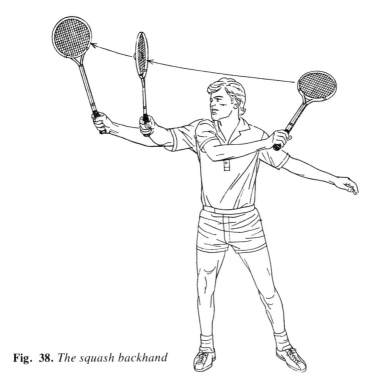

Fig. 38. *The squash backhand*

made with the ball. Most squash backhands are hit flat or with a little underspin. The continental type of grip will provide the slight opening of the racquet face that's needed for underspin, particularly on shots that are hit very low. On higher shots, the angle will be more closed, resulting in less underspin.

The racquetball backhand drive is almost a mirror-image of the forehand, with its extensive windup, wrist snap at contact with the ball and long, sweeping follow-through. As in squash, the backhand is a valuable shot, but many racquetballers are conspicuously weak on the backhand side. In racquetball, there is a little more time to run around the backhand, and you will always have the alternative of hitting a ceiling ball (Figure 39), so you can successfully avoid hitting backhands in many situations.

The backhand is best hit with a proper grip change (see Chapter 4) and by preparing properly so that body weight can be put into

Fig. 39. *The racquetball ceiling ball*

the shot, particularly for kill shots. The beginning racquetballer should exaggerate his movements in terms of stepping into the shot and snapping the wrist to get a feel for the need for power generation on the backhand. As in squash, the backhand cannot be strong-armed by using arm and wrist alone. The body has to be a component of the stroke.

Virtually all racquetball backhands should be hit flat, since underspin and topspin offer no special advantages. Some top players will use sidespin on their forehand and backhand drives, but this is an unnecessary complication for the novice and intermediate player. Until you reach a high standard in the sport, it's best to concentrate on getting enough wrist snap rather than using the wrist in different ways to put various kinds of spin on the ball. Perhaps even more than squash, wrist snap is the key to improving your play.

As with the forehand, the backhand is not a much used shot in badminton. If anything, the backhand is a more awkward stroke and is quite difficult for the novice player to execute with any accuracy. Since the net is so high, the shot must be hit around shoulder height, which results in a cramped movement of the arm and shoulder. Thus, the backhand relies on excessive wrist snap and support from the thumb for its effectiveness.

The racquet is taken back almost around the player's left ear and then swung in a semicircular motion across the body, making contact with the bird out in front. The wrist is severely cocked on the backswing to permit heavy wrist snap on contact. Follow-through on the backhand is quite long and tends to be downward, since this is the natural motion of the arm at this point.

A good player can use the sidearm backhand stroke with disguise to hit the bird either the length of the court or to drop into the forecourt. Such tactics call for control that is likely to be beyond the reach of the novice or lesser intermediate player. All in all, the badminton backhand drive is probably a stroke to be avoided by the less experienced player; and just as in platform tennis, a deep lob is often the best response.

The Overhead

The forehand and backhand drives tend to be the workhorse strokes of most of the racquet sports, but the overhead is a more sophisticated stroke. As a result, the overhead is often a way of judging a competent player. A good overhead is an essential part of a player's repertoire in four of our five major racquet sports, the exception being squash.

The tennis overhead, or smash, is a comparatively rare stroke, although it would be used more if only more players would learn the value of the lob in both singles and doubles. The overhead is the most common answer to the lob. It is a powerful stroke, executed with a motion like that of the serve. The smash is often intended to win the point outright. Thus, the overhead is an offensive shot that is usually hit hard.

When you are close to the net and your opponent hits a lob just over your reach, you will have to retreat a little, and perhaps jump, to hit an overhead. This is the most difficult type of smash, since it calls for extremely quick reactions and careful timing. This overhead gives the average player the most trouble, because he will rarely take the time to practice the shot and so develop the coordination it requires.

On the other hand, if your opponent hits a lob high and deep, you will have to retreat, often behind the baseline, to hit your smash. Since it is harder to hit a winning smash from deep in the court, it's best to let this ball bounce and hit the overhead after the bounce. The ball will be moving more slowly and you will have enough time to prepare correctly for your shot.

The stroke itself resembles the serving motion (see Figure 31), except that a long circular windup is not used. Instead, the racquet is taken directly back over the player's shoulder. The forward swing and wrist snap are similar to those needed for the serve. The major difference between contact for the two strokes is that spin is rarely used for the overhead. Since it is usually hit closer to the net, spin is not necessary. In addition, the objective is to hit the ball quite hard—spin would take a little off the pace of the overhead.

The overhead in tennis is very much an attacking shot. The player who uses the overhead will expect to win the point, and his opponent will probably be happy merely to get the ball back over the net. So after hitting an overhead, it's important to keep on the attack by closing in on the net, ready to finish out the point with your next shot should the first overhead be returned.

Although the overhead is a similar stroke in platform tennis and should be hit aggressively, it is not as much of an attacking shot. The smaller dimensions of the platform court increase the chances of the overhead being returned off the wires. In fact, an overhead that is hit too hard will come right off the wires and be an easy setup for a player used to screen play. So the platform overhead must often be hit more gently than the tennis smash.

In tennis, an overhead can often be hit at a sharp angle, so that it bounces high and out of reach of the opponent. That's generally not possible in platform tennis, since the ball will come back off the screens. The objective in platform play is to hit the ball deep to keep the opposing team away from the net. So the platform overhead is not as killing a shot as its tennis equivalent.

In a similar vein, platform tennis lobs are almost always hit on the fly (before the ball bounces), since there is neither room nor time to let a lob bounce. The team that lets a lob bounce will have to retreat even farther from the net to cover the lob, an undesirable move in platform play.

As you might expect, the overhead is frequently used in platform play, since you will be looking for ways to get the other team away from the controlling net position. So a platform player must have a competent overhead and be prepared to use it at all times. Fortunately, most lobs can be handled with a forehand overhead. The backhand overhead is even more of a rarity in platform than in regular tennis.

At the club level the platform overhead is hit without spin, since it simply isn't needed for control. Similarly, the majority of overheads should be hit deeply for safety. The sharply angled crosscourt smash is rarely used in platform, since the ball will rebound off the wires where it can easily be attacked.

The smash is a vital part of the stroking repertoire of the tennis and platform tennis player, but a squash player will rarely hit an overhead. That's because most of the play in squash consists of balls hit at a lower level. If a squash player is faced with a relatively high ball, it's usually sufficient to hit a high forehand or backhand volley or let the ball rebound from the back wall to hit a drive.

In racquetball, of course, high balls are an essential part of the game since the ceiling can be used, unlike squash. However, the overhead is rarely an attacking stroke as in tennis. Rather, the overhead is used to hit a ball up toward the ceiling—the ceiling ball (see Figure 39)—as a defensive maneuver. So the racquetball overhead is usually a defensive shot, like the lob in tennis.

Nonetheless, the ceiling ball is a very important shot in racquetball and is usually learned quickly by the novice player. The ceiling ball is hit with a motion similar to the tennis overhead, but the ball is taken more overhead than in front and is hit upward with a controlled wrist snap. The objective is to hit the ball with sufficient control for it to hit the ceiling quite close to the front wall, reach the front wall quite high and then rebound close to one of the sidewalls and drop deep in the court. It is often hit to the backhand side of the opposing player.

The ceiling ball may be hit on either the forehand or backhand side, but only the forehand ceiling ball is a true overhead shot. The backhand ceiling ball is like the basic backhand drive but with a very much higher point of contact and angle of direction.

Often a succession of ceiling balls will occur before one player commits the error that will allow his opponent to attempt a drive or a kill shot. So the overhead ceiling ball calls for a great deal of control to keep the ball from popping off the sidewall or sitting up in midcourt and giving the other player an easy return.

A hard smash to the front wall is almost never used in racquetball, since the ball would bounce high off the floor on its rebound and so be an easy target for the other player. There is no need to answer a lob with a smash, since a ceiling ball is easier and more reliable. In fact, the lob itself is not much used in racquetball. A badly hit lob will often produce an easy chance for a kill shot.

If the overhead is an important defensive shot in racquetball, it is a vital offensive and defensive shot in badminton. The several varieties of overhead form the most commonly used strokes in the sport. They are absolutely essential at any level of the game. The overhead is important because of the high net and the fact that the shuttlecock cannot bounce on the floor. Thus, almost all badminton play takes place above shoulder height, and contact with the bird should be made at or above that level.

The three major types of badminton overheads are the *smash,* a shot similar to the winning tennis stroke; the *drop,* a much gentler shot aimed at dropping the bird just over the net; and the *clear,* a high, deep shot that corresponds to the defensive lob of tennis and the ceiling ball of racquetball.

Although most badminton overheads could be hit off either the backhand or forehand side, owing to the nature of the game, most overhead strokes are forehands. If a shot comes up quickly on the backhand side, a player will often hit a forehand overhead "around the head," on the opposite side of the body, without too much difficulty.

Since three very different shots can be hit with the same basic overhead stroke, deception plays a very large part in badminton. Shots may be disguised until the very last fraction of a second. Changes in direction and pace can be made by altering the angle and direction of the wrist snap, which is so characteristic of badminton shots. However, there are some variations in timing of the three types of overheads.

For example, although all three are hit with a motion much like that of the tennis overhead, the badminton smash is hit well in front of the body, since the idea is to hit the bird down sharply into the opposing court. The sharper the angle, the more difficult the return. The overhead drop is hit in much the same way except very gently with less wrist snap. The overhead drop calls for careful touch—a slight error will give the opponent time to regain the attack.

The overhead clear (Figure 40), the main defensive shot in badminton, is hit when the bird is more directly overhead or even behind the player. The wrist snap is severe and used to send the bird high into the other court so it will drop almost vertically close to the backline. Naturally, a clear is often returned with another clear, since the objective is to get the opponent deep in the court so he cannot cover the entire court or hit down easily.

All three types of overhead are used in singles and doubles, but the drop and clear are more dangerous in doubles, since there is a likelihood of a player up front (to cover the drops) or deep (to

Fig. 40. *The badminton overhead clear*

cover the clears). So overhead shots tend to be more heavily used in singles play, where a succession of drops and deep clears will keep your opponent moving and tire him out very quickly.

The Lob

The lob is used in all our five major racquet sports as a way of gaining time. In tennis and platform tennis, the lob is also used to get the opponent away from the net.

There are two types of lob in tennis—the defensive, which is a high, arcing shot hit from the backcourt deep into the opponent's court, and the offensive lob, often hit from the midcourt area to be just out of reach of the opposing net player, to force him away from the net. Both shots tend to be much underused and yet they are two of the most useful shots in the sport.

The defensive lob is particularly valuable when you are drawn out of position and need time to get back into the point. A deep defensive lob will force your opponent to retreat and give you enough time to recover to the center of the baseline. The defensive lob is usually hit with a long, sweeping stroke like a forehand or backhand drive, but the racquet face is opened slightly and the racquet head comes up under the ball with a long and high follow-through. The shot may be hit equally well off either side, but the ball must go high and deep. A lob that falls short will provide an excellent opportunity for your opponent to hit an overhead smash and will not give you enough time to make your own recovery.

An offensive lob is an even more precise stroke in that it must be hit high enough to be beyond your opponent's reach, but yet not too high so that he has plenty of time to chase the ball down and smash it back, nor too low so he'll smash it from close to the net. An ideal offensive lob will drop rapidly in the backcourt so that your opponent cannot make an effective return. Some of the better players will hit an offensive lob with topspin so that the ball falls even more quickly into the backcourt and then kicks away sharply. Such a lob is virtually unreturnable. However, the topspin lob is an extremely difficult shot to hit, since its timing is very critical.

A newcomer to tennis would be well advised to learn how to lob right away, since many novices do not possess a usable overhead smash and, consequently, have no real reply to a lob. Thus the lob can be a winning shot against such a player. It is also especially useful in doubles against a team that persistently rushes the net. A few well-placed lobs early in the match will make such a team keep its distance from the net when they realize that they may have to beat a fast retreat to cover a lob.

The lob is equally useful in platform tennis, where it is almost always a defensive shot. The lob is an effective way of gaining time while waiting for a ball that can be attacked. And, of course, the lob will keep the opposing team away from the net. As a result, the lob is a frequently used shot in platform tennis. Unlike tennis, the platform tennis lob is not so vulnerable if hit short, since the overhead is not quite such a killing shot as in tennis.

Many lobs are hit from balls that come off the wires, because such balls must be taken in the backcourt, a defensive situation. The stroke itself is very much like the tennis stroke in that it resembles a forehand or backhand drive but is hit with a more open paddle face and contact is from under the ball. As noted earlier, the lob is the preferred shot on the backhand side. Some players even use the lob to return serve, a very rare occurrence in tennis.

The squash lob is used to gain time and to get an opponent off the T. The same basic forehand or backhand stroke is used for both high and low lobs, although the high shots don't have as much wrist snap. However, there are some high balls that perform the same function as the tennis lob. That is to say, these high shots will force a player back from the commanding center court position, thus allowing the other player to gain the center and retake the initiative.

Such loblike shots are hit high down the line to the front wall so they arc back close to the sidewall and bounce very close to the back wall, where they will be hard to return. However, these shots must be hit carefully or the ball will touch the ceiling (where it will be out of play) or may pop off the sidewall or back wall (making for an easy return by the opponent). Unlike tennis, a short lob is not a disaster, since it is difficult to hit a winner off a very high ball.

Lobs are more often used in the British version of the game with its softer ball and larger court. The lob is used more in the

North American game now with the introduction of the bouncier 70+ ball.

As mentioned in the last section on overheads, the ceiling ball of racquetball performs much the same function as the tennis lob. Although hit with an overhead motion, the ceiling ball is a high shot to the front wall designed to keep your opponent in the backcourt. As such, the ceiling ball is a defensive shot, like the defensive lob. Unlike squash, the ceiling ball is an important and frequently used racquetball shot.

As in squash, racquetball has loblike shots that hit high on the front wall and bounce deep into the backcourt. However, since the ceiling is used in play, players find that the ceiling ball is a much easier defensive shot and so prefer it to the almost total exclusion of the pure lob.

Badminton, too, does not have a lob by that name, but the clears perform the same function by forcing a player deep and giving you time to recover. Like the ceiling ball in racquetball, the overhead clear is probably the most frequently used defensive shot and, as such, is a staple in the badminton player's armory.

We have attempted to point out the significant differences and similarities in the strokes of our five sports to help you move from one sport to another. If, as we hope, you'd like to know more, we suggest that you consult one of the instruction books listed in the bibliography. Alternately, of course, talk to an expert or a teaching professional in the sport that has your interest.

Squash great Sharif Khan attacks a tennis ball as determinedly as he would a squash ball.

Racquetball champion Marty Hogan made a confident transition to squash for the 1979 World Racquets Championship.

Top-ranked tennis professional John McEnroe finds badminton as demanding a sport as tennis.

Ferocious concentration is a characteristic that racquetball pro Marty Hogan brings to his tennis game too.

Tennis players often find the angles of racquetball to be confusing, as John McEnroe evidently does here.

Guillermo Vilas, the Argentine tennis star, finds that topspin has its uses in table tennis.

The strokes may look a little unorthodox, but tennis star Bjorn Borg's fast footwork makes him a tough badminton player.

Like several formerly nationally ranked tennis players, Herb FitzGibbon has won national titles in platform tennis.

The defensive badminton serve is an unaccustomed motion for tennis pro Guillermo Vilas.

Chapter 7

How to Hit the Shorter Strokes

The Sophisticated Strokes

As we explained at the start of the last chapter, we have arbitrarily divided the strokes of our racquet sports into the longer and shorter types. In this chapter we will look at such strokes as the volley, the drop shot and the half-volley. We have also included the return of serve since, in many racquet sports, it is an abbreviated stroke because there is little time to get into position and hit a full ground stroke.

All the strokes covered in this chapter require a high degree of skill and are usually developed after the player has had considerable exposure to the sport. Almost all of the sports can be played without using the shorter strokes, but they become necessary when you are to play anything more than a defensive game. So you will need some of the shorter strokes as your level of play rises.

However, several of the shorter strokes are quite difficult to execute and so have a low chance of success. We think that you

123

should include them in your stroking repertoire but use them judiciously. The more variety you can add to your game, the better you will become as a racquet sports player. We suggest that you experiment with these strokes and practice them thoroughly before using them in competitive matches.

The Volley

In tennis the closeness of the net and the shortness of the swing make the volley one of the easiest of strokes. However, closer means quicker and more vulnerable, and these are obstacles to good volleying.

Of course, tennis can be played at all levels of the game without the volley. At the club level we see very little use of the volley in singles, and even in the professional game we seldom see Guillermo Vilas or Bjorn Borg move in to volley for the kill at the net.

In spite of the success of baseline players like Borg and Vilas, the amateur should use the volley because it is one of the most exciting and invigorating aspects of tennis and also a major tactical weapon. When Borg and Vilas do lose, it is usually to someone who comes to the net and finishes off the point with a well-played volley.

The volley grip varies with the skill level of the player. Club players usually hold the racquet with a forehand grip and switch to the backhand when they have time. Advanced players usually favor either a backhand or continental grip and, if time permits, may switch to a forehand grip when the ball comes to the forehand.

The forehand grip is not often used at the net by the better players because there isn't enough time to change grips, but also because underspin and not topspin is best when volleying. Underspin gives a player more control over the ball at the net, whereas topspin would give more of a margin for error over the net when playing from the backcourt.

The stroke on both the forehand and backhand is a half stroke, with the backswing being shortened for a kind of block and fol-low-through motion. While advanced players will usually take a full windup on a high and soft floating ball, the full swing is risky and should be used by the club player on only the easiest of setups. The club player may have difficulty recognizing soon enough which type of ball is coming to him, so it is better to use the half swing on all shots until one is consistent on all volleys.

The key to good tennis volleying is to turn sideways, taking the ball to the side rather than directly in front of the body. While there is often not time to turn the feet so they are parallel to the net, it is usually possible to at least turn the hips and shoulders.

In terms of court position, there are two types of volleys—the first volley and second volley. The first volley is usually taken around the service line and is generally hit deep in the court, often to the opponent's backhand. The second volley is usually made between the service line and the net, and there the idea is to volley the ball away, because the angles are better for short shots or quick thrusts to the baseline.

Volleying is an offensive tactic whose primary purpose is to rush an opponent into an error. Therefore, you should be coming to the net to hit a winner, because if you don't, your opponent won't rush and you'll provide him with an easy target to pass. If you don't finish off your opponent with the first two volleys, your offensive net position can easily turn into a precarious defensive one.

The volley is one of platform tennis's essential strokes, be-cause dominating the net position is the key to winning platform tennis. It is difficult to dominate the net without a volley.

Intermediate platform players will hit most volleys with the forehand, so they will most often use a forehand grip. However, top platform players use the backhand or continental grip for all volleys, but they will attempt to take as many volleys as they can with the backhand. The game is really too quick to change grips on the volley, and because the backhand volley is more flexible than the forehand, it is the easier of the two shots for experienced players. The forehand volley can cover only the area from the full extension of the arm to the hip on the side of your hitting arm. Any ball hit directly at you (which is where most drives seem to go) cannot be volleyed with the forehand. The backhand volley (Figure 41), however, can cover an area extending from the hip of your hitting arm side to a full extension of the arm across the body, which includes the shots hit directly at your body.

The closer you are to the net, the easier it is to volley, so the more effective your volley will be. Therefore, when you see the opposition winding up to drive the ball, both you and your partner should move in to be on top of the net, with the partner on the side nearest the ball covering the down-the-line shot, and the partner farthest from the ball covering the center of the court. You can leave the sharp crosscourt uncovered because there is so little room on a platform court to make that shot.

Fig. 41. *The platform tennis backhand volley*

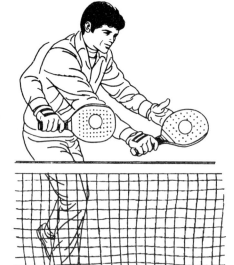

Obviously, when you are not sure if the opposition is going to lob or drive, you can't move so close to the net. However, you can often play much closer to the net than in tennis, because a lob over the players' heads is not as easy in platform as it is in tennis.

Unlike tennis, in platform tennis you go to the net to play steady. It is almost impossible to hit a volley winner with two opponents covering such a small court. If you try, you'll just make a lot of unforced errors. It is even more difficult for the backcourt team to get a ball by the net team, so you should let the baseline team make the errors trying to pass. You should be able to hit overheads and volleys more easily and consistently than the opposition can hit lobs and drives, so play it steady at net—the odds are heavily in favor of the net team winning the point.

In racquetball the volley, called a "fly ball" or "fly kill" when a winner is hit, is rarely used. The large court, small racquet and fast ball make it very difficult to cut off shots coming directly off the wall before the ball has bounced. However, when the volley is hit, the forehand grip is usually used on both sides, because that is the grip that is held when waiting for a ball. The volley situation usually comes up in a hurry, and there is just no time to switch grips. Because the ball is moving rapidly, the volley is often a slap shot without a full windup. The shorter racquet allows you to take a bigger swing than in tennis, but a full windup as used on the ground strokes is usually not possible.

The volley is either hit in front of your opponent or when you are moving from behind him toward the front wall. Your strategy should be to rush your opponent and hit the ball before he has time to get set.

The squash volley is hit using one grip, as are all the squash shots. The typical squash grip is between the backhand grip and the continental.

Volleying in squash is more frequent than in racquetball because the court is smaller, the ball deader and the racquet longer. However, because the racquet is longer, the volley is stroked without a full windup, but with a longer swing than in tennis.

Wrist snap is often used to add power, but not as much as in a normal ground stroke. Usually a volley is a rushed shot, and the long racquet and small head make for frequent mis-hits, so the swing should be much more controlled than on the ground strokes.

The volley is usually hit from in front of your opponent or as you are moving from behind toward the front wall. The purpose of the volley is to keep or take the T while keeping your opponent behind you.

In badminton, everything but the overhead is, in a sense, a volley because every shot in this game is taken before the shuttlecock bounces. Therefore, we will liken the volley to net shots in badminton, which are those hit from a position close to the net. In singles, these shots should be made as close to the net as possible, because your opponent will have less time to cover your return and because you should hit the shuttlecock when it is above the net.

Grips for these shots are the same as for the regular forehand or backhand drive. The stroke is made with the racquet well out in front and the wrist laid back, to "hold" the opponent for a last-minute change of direction or a "bump" straight ahead. On these shots you can't just stick your racquet out and hold it firm, as in tennis. Instead, the shuttlecock must be "bumped" or "bounced" off the racquet to give it forward motion.

The net shots are usually drop shots used either to hit an outright winner or as a means of forcing your opponent to hit up. In either case, disguise through the delicate use of the wrist and little or no backswing or follow-through is required. Body position is not critical as long as you can control the shuttlecock with your wrist and the arm is well extended in front of you.

If the shuttlecock is taken at or above the top of the net, it can be hit down toward an open part of the court. If the bird is taken below the top of the net, it should be hit straight up and over the net if your opponent is deep in the court. If your opponent has moved in and hit a drop shot very close to the net, you should return the shuttlecock along the top of the net.

In doubles, the play is so fast that there is often no time to even switch grips, much less change strokes. Therefore, a Western or frying-pan grip is often used, and the racquet head is held straight up in the air. Any loose shot that is short and above the net should be flicked with the wrist at a sharp angle to the ground. As with the tennis volley, this shot is used to finish off the point.

The Drop Shot

Good tennis can be played without the drop shot since it is not an important tactical weapon. The drop shot is a tool that should be used sparingly, so the threat of its use is always present in your opponent's mind. However, if the drop shot is used too often, a smart player will start to anticipate it and will come in and frequently put the ball away.

The best players often use a backhand or continental grip for both forehand and backhand drops. This allows the shot to be hit with underspin, which tends to make the ball bounce lower and not carry forward. Underspin also allows the ball to stay on the racquet longer, which provides more control or "touch." If the drop shot is not hit with perfect control, you'll hit it too far beyond the net and probably lose the point.

The stroke itself is usually an abbreviated ground stroke, with a shorter backswing and follow-through. Disguise is important, so good players try to prepare as they would for a normal ground stroke, changing speed and direction by either sliding under the ball or just patting the ball after taking the customary windup.

The drop shot should be hit only when you are in control of the point. To try a delicate drop when you are being pressed deep in the backcourt is to gamble wildly. Drop shots are best executed from well inside the baseline and off a ball that you could hit deep to the baseline. There are two key factors for a good drop shot: firstly, *disguise*—make the opponent think you are going to hit a deep drive; and secondly, *time*—the closer you are to the net, the shorter your shot will be, so your opponent will have less time to see the shot and get to the ball before it bounces a second time.

The drop shot does not exist in platform tennis. Short shots are made only by the volleyer, who usually tries to drop the ball over the net or angle it short into the screens, and then only when he is right on top of the net.

Some players with very unorthodox grips can hit a stop volley, in which a hard-hit drive is "stopped" by the volleyer so that all speed is absorbed on the racquet and the ball just drops over the net, but it is not a stroke to be recommended.

Whereas the tennis drop shot is usually a soft touch shot that just floats over the net, the fast, bouncy ball of racquetball makes such touch shots impossible, because your opponent will always run them down and thus leave you vulnerable. Drop shots in racquetball should be hit very firmly, with a full swing. The grip may be either forehand or backhand, depending on which side the ball is hit. A racquetball drop shot will work no matter how hard you hit it, as long as it stays low. Drop shots are most easily made in the corner, where there are two walls to absorb the speed of the ball and change its direction, but straight drops off the front wall can also work if they are hit extremely low.

Drop shots are best hit when your opponent is behind you, and so farther from the ball, but they can also be hit from behind your opponent as long as the shot is well disguised.

Good racquetball, tennis and platform tennis can be played without the drop shot, but not squash. At the tournament level of squash play, the drop is one of the prime shots in setting your opponent up for the kill. While even a good drop shot will be run down by an opponent who is in shape, he will then be close to the front wall and very vulnerable for the next shot.

In squash, the drop shot stroke should be disguised to look exactly like a drive, with a full backswing and wrist cock.

The shot is best hit from in front of your opponent, but it can also be hit effectively from behind the T. As in racquetball, there are two basic drop shots—the straight drop and the corner drop. The latter is easier to hit. Both these shots should be made with quick, firm strokes. The tennislike floater will probably be run down and attacked, because the ball will be moving so slowly through the air that your opponent will have time to recover even if caught off balance. A good drop shot should be hit firmly and be well disguised.

The badminton drop shot can be either a net shot or hit deeper in the court with an overhead or a ground stroke. Like squash, good badminton cannot be played without the drop shot. The drop shot serves not only to hit winners into the open part of the court, but also to set your opponent up by making him hit up.

The "redrop" is often used in answer to a drop shot and is a short delicate wrist shot with little or no arm swing usually made from below the net. The best redrop is usually straight ahead, because it gives your opponent the least amount of time.

The overhead drop is the most frequently used offensive drop shot and is hit in the same way as the overhead clear or smash, but the racquet head does not go through the shuttlecock with the same speed. At the last instant, the wrist is relaxed and the arm slows almost to a stop as the shuttlecock is contacted. The purpose of hitting the drop shot like a smash or clear is disguise. The shuttlecock will be moving quite slowly on a drop shot, even though it is hit firmly, so a good player will have more time to reach this shot than a smash. So your opponent must be deceived with disguise.

The less offensive drop shots (Figure 42), hit at chest or knee level, should also be disguised. Always make your opponent think you are going to hit a power shot, either a drive or a clear, by always using the same preparation and backswing before hitting a drop shot. Disguise is especially important the deeper you are in the court.

While the drop shot is one of the most important shots in badminton, it must not be overused. Your opponent will soon begin to anticipate the drop and leave you in a vulnerable position with his net shots.

To further disguise overhead drop shots, slice or reverse spin is used by advanced players. These shots are more risky than flat

Fig. 42. *The badminton underhand drop shot*

drops, because a smaller portion of the racquet face is presented to the shuttlecock, so only players with excellent racquet control should attempt them.

More than in any other of our games the purpose of badminton is to move the opponent and make him hit up. A well-disguised drop shot accomplishes this objective very effectively and therefore, unlike in our other sports, must be understood and mastered to become a good badminton player.

The Half-Volley

The half-volley, a ground stroke hit immediately after the ball bounces, is a shot that is rarely used in tennis except by those players who serve and volley and have to hit the ball near their feet. The half-volley is one of the most difficult shots to hit properly and should be avoided if at all possible. If you find you are

132

half-volleying a great deal, you are not following your serve to net quickly enough. You should change your strategy to avoid half-volleying.

The grip is usually a continental or backhand for both sides. The shot has a low and very abbreviated backswing. Like the volley, it is a block and follow-through stroke (Figure 43).

If you have to half-volley in platform tennis, you are in real trouble. The stroke is the same as in tennis, but the court is so small that it's even more difficult to control this shot. If you find you are using this shot more than a few times a set, you'd better change your strategy.

A half-volley in racquetball is also an infrequently used shot; but different from platform and tennis, it is a shot that may be used deliberately to rush an opponent by taking advantage of an opening that might close if a conventional stroke were used. The shot is usually used when in front of an opponent or when an opponent is in front of you but has just hit a weak shot.

Fig. 43. *The tennis half-volley*

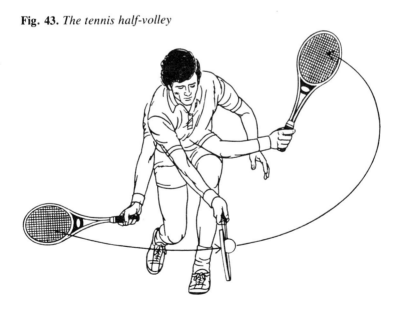

The grips are the same as for the forehand and backhand drives, but the stroke does not have to be executed as carefully as in tennis or platform tennis. This is because the ball does not have to clear a net and the racquet is shorter and easier to control.

As in racquetball, the squash half-volley is not played often but is hit deliberately to rush an opponent. The half-volley is a more carefully executed shot than its racquetball counterpart, with little or no wrist snap. The shot can be played in front of or behind an opponent, but when you are behind an opponent you should choose a more powerful shot to get the ball past your opponent.

Since the shuttlecock can't bounce, there is no equivalent of a half-volley in badminton.

The Return of Serve

The return of serve at the top level of tennis is one of the finer arts of sports. If Ken Rosewall or Jimmy Connors were baseball players, both would be among the game's top hitters. The ball is often moving toward them at speeds approaching those achieved by the great baseball fastballers, but there is no batter's box. Imagine how tough the game would be if you had to place your serve between Connors' knees and armpits and less than a racquet length away from him.

The tennis return-of-serve stroke will vary with the speed and direction of the serve. Whether you have time for a full backswing or just a block, the most critical thing is to turn the body. Even if the feet cannot be positioned properly, the hips and shoulders must be turned by all players with good returns of serve.

The platform tennis return of serve is not usually hit with a shorter swing, but it can be considered half a shot in that the backhand is rarely used to return serve. All the top players hit forehands almost exclusively. Should the receiver have to take the ball on the backhand, the return is almost always lobbed.

The serve is usually the maximum point of vulnerability, so good players try to create as much pressure as possible by driving the return with the most potent weapon—the forehand. To allow the server to serve to your backhand is to lesson the pressure on him and allow the serving team to more easily establish the net position.

In racquetball, the return of serve can often be just a lunge and flick off an opponent's driving first serve, so it is often a shorter stroke. The objective is to keep the return deep and preferably to your opponent's backhand. Don't try anything tricky or aggressive unless the serve is a weak one that leaves you in good position.

For squash, the return of serve (Figure 44) directly off the front wall or sidewall is quite similar to a volley. The backswing is relatively short and the wrist is often held quite firm because of the accuracy required on the return of serve.

Fig. 44. *The squash backhand return of serve*

A good lob serve in squash will be falling after it comes off the sidewall. The timing of the return of such a shot is quite critical, so it is important to face the wall, watch the ball very closely and take an abbreviated swing. Otherwise, this shot can be easily mis-hit. The ball is hit with a sweeping action of the arm rather than a snap of the wrist. This techinque will help you time the ball properly and achieve the accuracy that is so important.

In badminton doubles, the return of serve is often charged, so that the receiver can catch the shuttlecock before it has fallen and so hit it close to the net and angled down sharply. For this shot a Western grip is used, with the racquet head held straight up, much in the manner of a net shot in doubles. Rushing the serve allows little time for grip or stroke change, so the Western grip is preferred. The serve is not often rushed in singles, because the longer serving area makes the short serve unnecessary.

Chapter 8

The Strategies of the Racquet Sports

Similar Tactics

Although, as we've seen in the last two chapters, the racquet sports often use different strokes, there are many parallels that can be drawn in tactics and strategies. In each of the games, there are clearly situations where, all else being equal, one player will have control. In tennis, for example, the player at the net has control. In squash, the player on the T has control. And so on for our other sports.

This chapter will attempt to show you the strategies for each sport. First, we'll give you our ten commandments, which apply, pretty much without exception, to all our five major racquet sports. Then we'll take a look at each of the sports and give you ideas for your game plans in those sports.

Of course, the particular tactics that you use in your sports may vary from our suggestions. We realize that ability comes into play here. An older tennis player, for example, will not rush the net after serving quite so frequently as a young player who is fleet

137

of foot and has plenty of stamina. You will have to adapt our ideas to your own game, knowing your own limitations in that particular sport.

The Ten Commandments of the Racquet Sports

1. *Thou shalt not make unnecessary errors:* This is the first and the greatest of the racquet sports laws. All the racquet games are sufficiently difficult that it's best to give your opponent a chance to miss rather than risking an error yourself. While the great Bill Tilden was talking about tennis when he enunciated the first rule of racquet tactics, it can be applied to any of our sports: "Keep the ball in play and give your opponent another shot at it, rather than risk the error by taking an unnecessary chance."

In other words, simply get the ball back so your opponent can make the error. How many times have you seen a player go for a winner and make an error? The booming overhead doesn't look so good if it crashes into the net when a less flamboyant and higher percentage shot would have been enough to force an error.

Tennis and platform tennis are games in which far more errors are made than winners. Racquetball and squash matches usually have more winners than errors, except for novice players. Badminton falls somewhere in the middle, with winners usually slightly exceeding errors. But even though the games vary in the frequency with which attacking shots can be logically attempted, this rule still applies to each game.

2. *Love thy opponent's weakness as thyself:* Once you have enough ball control, you can begin working on an opponent's weakness. For example, in all our sports the backhand is almost always weaker than the forehand. Thus, in tennis, badminton and racquetball in particular, the backhand should be the focal point of both your offense and your defense.

While the backhand is usually less powerful in squash than the forehand, especially at the club level, there are other weaknesses that may be easier to exploit, such as court coverage and stamina. Squash matches are often won because one player is in better shape, so it may be more important to keep an opponent moving from side to side rather than concentrating on his backhand.

In platform tennis, hitting to the opposition's backhand will produce a lob rather than an error, even though the backhand is much weaker than the forehand in this game. But there are other weaknesses in platform play, the most common being the serve. With only one serve, and the absolute necessity of following it to net, the serve is the most vulnerable time for the offensive team. The serve should be attacked by the receiver as much as possible.

While the weakness may vary with the sport or the opposition, one is always present, and should be exploited.

3. *Thou shalt have no other god but depth:* If you can consistently keep the ball deep, two things will happen: your opponent will be forced to back up, making it more difficult for him to cover the entire court; and he will hit up rather than down. In any racquet sport, it is preferable to hit down, because that allows you to control the court better and rushes your opponent more.

Hitting deep in tennis is perhaps the most difficult strategy to follow, because it implies a level of consistency that not many of us have. A good technique for achieving consistent depth is to pick a height over the net, and aim for it. Six to ten feet of clearance will usually give good depth from the baseline but, of course, the height will vary with your exact court position and speed of shot.

In badminton, depth is vital, since a player close to the net often will be able to hit down on the bird and so win the point. A player who is kept back will usually play less aggressively and will often hit overhead clears, in turn, to keep his opponent away from the net and to avoid hitting a short shot that can be put away very easily.

In platform tennis, depth on the serve is more important than on the ground strokes. A short serve, even if it is hard and well spun, invites attack, because it allows the receiver to hit down while moving forward. The ball can be hit awfully hard and still stay in the court when the receiver is hitting down. In addition, the shorter the serve, the sooner it is hit, which means the server has less time to get to net and the net man has less time to protect himself.

A key objective of racquetball and squash is to keep your opponent behind you, so your shots should be hit deep, preferably to the back wall but not so hard as to bounce off it. This forces your opponent out of position, making him vulnerable to short shots and forcing him to hit up, an angle that makes hitting a winner difficult. If his return is short and high, you can then hit down for a low front wall or corner winner. Of course, in a wall game, if you hit down too sharply, the ball will come up, so experienced players let the ball drop somewhat before hitting for the winner.

4. *Thou shalt not take the down-the-line in vain:* This law demands that you understand the angles—how to open up your opponent's court and how to protect your own court in the most efficient manner. Crosscourt shots may produce fewer errors on your part, but they also give your opponent more time, improve his angles, give you more court to cover and, unless hit well, leave you very vulnerable to attack.

When attacking in tennis, approach shots as you go to the net should usually be hit down the line (Figure 45), preferably from your forehand to your opponent's backhand. Crosscourt approach shots should be avoided, because they open up the side of the court away from you and usually pass closer to your opponent. So attack down the line and cover the down-the-line passing shot.

When you're in the backcourt, tennis crosscourt returns give you more time to get back into position and you have more court to aim for, but they make you very vulnerable to the down-the-line attack. The same is true of badminton.

The object of squash and racquetball is to dominate the center of the court while keeping your opponent behind you. Thus, the rail shot (Figure 46) helps you to maintain or achieve that position, because it goes past your opponent more quickly than the

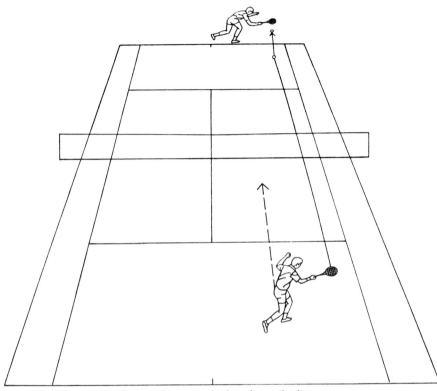

Fig. 45. *Tennis: forehand approach shot down the line*

crosscourt shot. Unlike the crosscourt, this down-the-line shot will not draw your opponent toward the center of the court. A poorly executed crosscourt shot not only costs you position but also provides the opposition with a wider range of angles of attack.

If you find yourself behind your opponent, the down-the-line shot will pass him more quickly than the crosscourt, and does not have to be hit as precisely to obtain your objective of getting in front.

When a team is at net in platform tennis, the down-the-line is

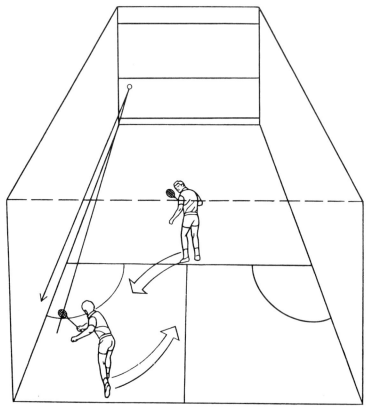

Fig. 46. *Squash: backhand rail shot to draw opponent off the T*

covered by the player nearest the ball, and the center court shots
are covered by the player farthest from the ball. If a player tried
to cover more than one angle, he might not be able to react
quickly enough to cover any shot. Therefore, leave the sharp
crosscourt uncovered, and make little allowance for the offensive
lob.

5. *It is more blessed to hit early than late:* This law refers to
the time at which you take the ball, not its position relative to the
body. By taking the ball early, either on the rise, on the volley or

142

in front of your opponent, you give your opponent less time to react, making it easier to penetrate his defense or to catch him off guard with a short shot. This applies to all our racquet sports.

6. *Honor your good shots by moving forward:* Whenever you hit a forcing ground stroke, move forward. This is true even in tennis and platform tennis when the opposition is at the net. Invariably, a low hard passing shot in these two games is returned short in the court, so move forward in order to catch the return near the top of its bounce.

In squash and racquetball, hard and accurate down-the-line and crosscourt shots are desirable not only because they get the opposition out of position but because they allow you to move ahead of your opponent. Back up after hitting a good ground stroke in any of these games and you will lose much of the impact of your shot.

7. *Thou shalt kill when you have the opportunity:* If you don't attack when your opponent provides an opening (Figure 47), you will be wasting an opportunity. In addition, you won't be putting any pressure on your opponent, because he'll have no fear of hitting high or short. Therefore, not only will you be wasting your opportunity but your opponent will have little pressure that might make unforced errors.

8. *Thou shalt cover the center of the court:* In squash and racquetball, your shots should be hit so you can command the center of the court. In tennis and platform tennis, you shouldn't stand in the midcourt, but you do want to hit as many balls as you can from this position. Balls that bounce short near the middle of the platform tennis or tennis court give you a great attacking opportunity. The player who hits the ball from midcourt is in an excellent attacking position to go up to the net.

9. *Honor thy defense as well as thy offense:* It is important to recognize that during the ebb and flow of a point, you can continually move from offense to defense, and your shots should be chosen based on which phase you are in. In tennis, for instance, if your opponent suddenly whacks a sharply angled forehand, pulling you out of position, you should realize you are suddenly

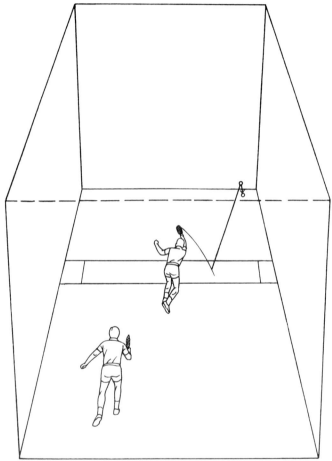

Fig. 47. *Racquetball: the kill shot from the center court position*

on the defensive. Now, you should throw up a semilob to give yourself time to get back in position. To try to answer a good shot with a better one risks an unforced error. The only time a really good shot should be answered with an attempted better one is when you are hopelessly out of position.

Even in the ultimate offensive game, professional racquetball, defense can play a vital role. In the finals of the 1978 national championships, Marty Hogan was leading Charlie Brumfield by one game and 13 to 5 in the second. At this point Brumfield went to the defensive ceiling ball, while Hogan, the greatest shooter of all time, made error after error by trying for winners off of Brumfield's deep ceiling balls. Brumfield surged ahead 20 to 16, only to have Hogan suddenly get hot again and nip Brumfield 21 to 20.

When you are getting the best of a rally, you should not suddenly use a defensive shot. Keep the pressure on when you have the upper hand.

10. *Thou shalt not covet thy opponent's game:* Put simply, don't be overawed by your opponent's game when you take to the court, even if he is clearly better than you. It is far better to focus on how you are going to play him, given the strengths of his game and the limitations of your own, than on how good he is. Just remember, the world of racquet sports has seen far greater upsets than you beating your club champion.

Two matches come to mind where the better player, and heavy favorite, left the court a loser because of clever strategy on the part of the opposition. The first was in 1975 when Arthur Ashe upset Jimmy Connors in the Wimbledon finals. In this match Ashe chose to abandon his usual power game, even though they were playing on one of the world's fastest surfaces, for spins and off-speed shots to blunt the ferocious power of Connors.

Connors lost another important final, this time the 1977 U.S. Open, because Guillermo Vilas abandoned his topspin backhand after losing the first set. Putting aside his best shot, he began using an underspin backhand, a shot he rarely uses, in order to attack Connors' weak low forehand. The change in tactics worked, and Vilas won in four sets.

So next time you go onto the court, don't fret about winning or losing; just concentrate on how you are going to play your opponent. It will not only help your concentration but help you to relax.

Your Racquet Sports Game Plans

Tennis: Defense or Offense

When you first begin to play tennis, most of your game will be played from the backcourt, trading ground strokes with your opponent. This is largely a defensive game where you merely get the ball back and wait for your opponent to make an error. It can be seen at its highest level in the game of Chris Evert, a consummate ground-stroker who rarely hits an error but keeps the pressure on her opponents so that they are forced into making errors.

Of course, it isn't enough merely to get the ball back. If you hit a short ball, your opponent may come up to the net and put your next shot away with a sharply placed volley. You must hit deep when you are playing on the baseline, and you should move your opponent about to open up the court and increase the chances of forcing an error. And if your opponent hits a short ball, you should be ready to advance on the net, where you'll be able to make a winning volley.

At a higher level of tennis, whether singles or doubles, you will realize that control of the game comes from holding the net position. Thus, you will often follow your serve to the net or, if you are playing from the baseline, look for the short ball that will let you hit an approach shot and come to the net. Once at the net, you will be able to hit more angled shots, and so increase the chances of your winning the point.

The defense against the net player is, of course, the lob over the player's head or accurate passing shots. Thus, the lob is an essential shot for doubles play or in singles when the players go to the net frequently.

Platform Tennis: Quick on the Offensive

Although platform tennis resembles conventional tennis in strategic terms, the overriding principle is to gain control of the net. Even though a player is allowed only one serve, he should follow his serve to the net every time. This will put both team members close to the net, each covering his own half of the court. A team that can get to the net and stay there will usually win the point. Thus, there are virtually no baseline rallies in platform tennis, although the lob is used frequently to force the opponents away from the net.

The distinguishing factor between tennis and platform tennis is the wire screens that can be used to keep the ball in play. If you are away from the net and an opponent hits a hard shot, don't attempt to return it right away. Let the ball come off the screen, where it will lose more than 50 percent of its speed (a lot more if it bounces off two screens). You can then return the ball with a relatively easy lob (Figure 48). Your only problem will be in judging the rebound of the ball, especially if you are a former tennis player. Squash and racquetball players will have less difficulty.

After lobbing off the screens, get into position to attack an overhead with your forehand. Remember that your lobs have to be well placed to be successful in platform play. A short or low lob will be an easy overhead for the other team.

Badminton: Speed and Touch

Badminton is much more of an attacking game than tennis but not such a straightforward "killing" game as racquetball. If there is one strategic key in badminton, it is to make your opponent hit up. In general, the player who has to hit up will lose and the player who hits down will win the point. The objective is to force your opponent to hit up so you can then hit down for a winner. Thus, a deep serve in singles is usually more effective than a

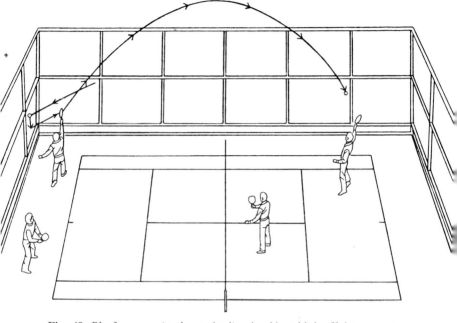

Fig. 48. *Platform tennis: down-the-line backhand lob off the screens*

Fig. 49. *Badminton: use of the overhead clear in mixed doubles*

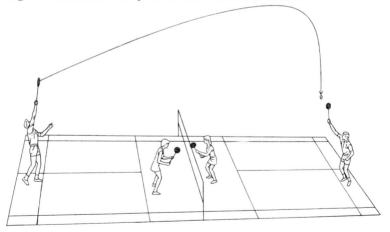

short serve, since the receiver will have to hit up from the back-court to return deep.

However, the tactics of badminton vary according to the type of game—singles, doubles or mixed doubles. In singles, the deep serve will force the opponent back and allow the server to keep control of the midcourt area. The receiver will often hit overhead clears to get his opponent away from the midcourt or drop shots to force him to rush to the net. In either case, the player is looking for a high return that can be smashed to win the point.

In mixed doubles, a common version of the sport, it's usual for the woman to play close to the net and the man to play deep (Figure 49). This results in shorter rallies than in singles play. However, as in tennis, the key is to go for the weakness—of either player. The weakness must be attacked to force an error or to win the point directly.

In regular doubles, both players defend from the midcourt area, each covering his own half of the court. As they move into the attack, they may adopt a version of the one-up, one-back formation, but not quite so precisely aligned as for mixed play. For example, if one player retreats to smash a deep clear, the other partner will move toward the net, as in the mixed formation. But if forced back on the defensive, both players will take up a side-by-side position. However, the basics are the same—you should try to force the opponents to hit up so that you can close in and hit down to win the point with a smash.

Squash: A Game of Position

The controlling position in squash is the "T" formed by the service line and the center line between the two service boxes. Possession of the T means control of the point. Although a player will leave the T frequently to return a ball, it's the position to which he will return as quickly as possible to stay on top of the point.

Of course, the converse of keeping the T position is to make sure that your opponent has difficulty gaining the T himself. To do just that you must aim your shots so the ball does not hit the sidewall until it has passed the T. If you are going for the back corners, you must hit deep drives that will pull your opponent off the T. You must also learn to control the ball, since overhitting will make the ball bounce off the back wall for a much easier return than if your shot just dies in the back corner.

When your opponent is pushed into one of the back corners, then you can go for one of the front corners with a drop shot or a corner shot that will be a winner. Squash resembles badminton in that the objective is to set up a winning situation. Rallies may be very long between two competent players of similar ability. Squash at that level becomes a game of consistency. The player who can place the ball consistently well will most often win the game.

In squash, you will be probing for a weak return. When that return comes, you must take the opportunity and go for the winner. Unlike tennis, the majority of squash points are not won on errors at the top level. Squash is more often won on winners set up by forcing a weak return that can then be put away. In many ways, squash is like a circular game of fencing. The players rotate in and out of the T position looking for the opening that will give a winning shot. Although squash often looks to the uninitiated like a power game, it is in fact a game of finesse—in both stroking and strategy.

Racquetball: The Killer's Game

More than any of our other racquet sports, racquetball is a game of winners at any level beyond that of the novice. To beat your opponent, you must be prepared to look for the opening and then go for the winning shot. Most often this will be a drive low to the front wall that comes off so low it is unreturnable—the "kill shot" in racquetball parlance. Players who can kill the ball accurately—the "shooters"—are most likely to be successful racquetballers.

The key to winning racquetball is control of the center court position—the area in the center of the court just a few steps behind the short line. It's the equivalent of the T in squash and comparable to playing at the net in tennis or platform tennis. In the center court position you are almost the same distance from all four corners, which cuts down on the time taken to reach your opponent's ball.

To get a player away from the center court, you must hit down the sides of the court with shots that go deep but do not rebound significantly from the back wall (a rebounding ball will give an easy setup to your opponent). The most frequently used defense is the ceiling ball, which, in turn, results in another ceiling ball. Such rallies can be quite long, with each player waiting for the other to hit the ball short or too hard so that it presents a chance for a drive or a kill shot.

Finesse shots such as the drop and "nick" shots of squash are not much used in racquetball because the ball is too bouncy. The slightest error in hitting a drop shot will cause the ball to bounce out into the court where it can be dealt with summarily. This often means the younger power players have a distinct advantage in racquetball. Nonetheless, power often comes at the expense of accuracy, so a less powerful player can make up for the lack by having greater accuracy. Even so, such a player must go for the kill when the opportunity arises.

Racquetballers often seem to hit a hot streak—a succession of winning kills. If that happens to your opponent, the only thing to do is wait it out. Eventually, the power player will lose a little accuracy so you can pour on the pressure.

Chapter 9

The Other Racquet Sports

Court Tennis

The ancient sport of court tennis is the grandfather of all the racquet games, dating back to medieval times. Today, court tennis is probably the least popular of all the racquet sports, since there are very few courts available. With only eight courts in the United States and perhaps twenty or so worldwide, there are only a few thousand people who know how to play the game and perhaps a few hundred regular players.

Interestingly enough, court tennis has some of the characteristics of all of our racquet sports. It is played on an indoor court, deriving from the courtyard of a castle. The court is divided by a net, as in tennis and badminton, but the walls can be used, as in squash and racquetball. The racquet looks somewhat like a tennis racquet but is heavier and has a slightly lopsided head. The ball is heavier than a tennis ball and is quite solid.

The ball is put into play with a serve that runs along the roof of a gallery alongside the court (called the "penthouse") and then rolls off to land in a service box. Wristy strokes are used to produce lots of underspin so that the ball skids off the court and rebounds short off the back wall. Scoring is similar to that of

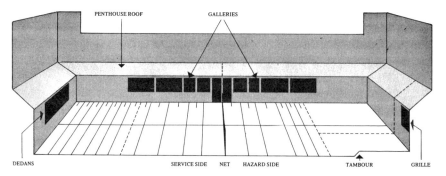

DEDANS SERVICE SIDE NET HAZARD SIDE TAMBOUR GRILLE

PENTHOUSE ROOF GALLERIES

Fig. 50. *The game of court tennis*

regular tennis but with the addition of some arcane rules involving what are called "chases." By precise placement of the ball, one player can defer the decision of a point to a new situation—the chase. It is this feature of court tennis that has caused comparisons with chess.

Unfortunately, we do not have the space to go into court tennis in detail. Suffice it to say that court tennis is one of the most intriguing of the racquet sports and quite possibly the most complex. As a racquet sports player you are likely to be fascinated by the game, but unfortunately it is unlikely that you'll have the opportunity to play.

More information on the sport of court tennis can be obtained from the U.S. Court Tennis Association, The Racquet and Tennis Club, 370 Park Avenue, New York, N.Y. 10022.

Hard Rackets

The game of hard rackets (or just "rackets") developed from a game played against the wall of London's Fleet Street debtors' prison. Later, the game was adopted by some of England's top private schools and eventually became a sport for the Victorian well-to-do in England. Nowadays, there are few rackets courts left, perhaps ten in the United States, and only a few hundred

154

serious players in this country. The game still has a following in the English private schools and a few universities.

Rackets is played in an enormous court, 60 feet long by 30 feet wide, with a front wall that is 30 feet high. It's easy to see why rackets courts are no longer being built. The racquets are similar to squash racquets but slightly longer. The balls are only an inch in diameter and are extremely hard. Only one maker of racquets and another of balls are left in England.

The game itself is similar to squash but the ball must be hit very hard and travels at incredible speeds (150 mph or more). The speeds are so high that the game can be very dangerous, especially for the beginner.

Rackets has been called the most exciting of all the racquet sports. The game places a premium on speed and power. Although the rallies are shorter than for squash, the games often

Fig. 51. *The game of hard rackets*

William Surtees

last longer since only the server can score points. Thus, rackets is also a game where stamina counts.

As with court tennis, the game is appealing to anyone who has ever played one of the wall sports, but the chances of playing the game are slim. For more information on the sport, write North American Rackets Association, 1430 Lake Shore Drive, Chicago, Ill. 60610.

Frontennis

The game of frontennis is a direct descendant of the Basque game of pelota, from which the sport of jai alai is also derived. Like jai alai, frontennis is played in a three-sided court, approximately 125 feet long by 36 feet wide, with walls 30 feet high. One long side of the court is open to the spectators, who are shielded from the fast-moving ball by a screen or net.

Fig. 52. *The game of frontennis*

Unlike jai alai, which is played with Basque "cestas," which look like long, thin wicker baskets, frontennis is played with specially reinforced tennis racquets loosely strung with a thick nylon string. The ball is about the size of a golf ball, quite hard and extremely fast.

Most of the U.S. frontennis courts or "frontons" are located in Florida, where the game is popular with Cuban emigrés, or in Arizona, where the game has a strong Mexican influence. Although there are only a few thousand players in the United States, the game is popular in Mexico and Spain.

The game itself is easier than squash and resembles racquetball. Most of the shots are taken around chest or shoulder height. The key to the game is to keep the ball hugging the left wall where it has to be hit on the backhand. It is most often played as a doubles game with one man up front and one deep. The deep player will take most of the shots and must be a steady player. The front court player has to be fast (and fearless).

If you live in the South and would like to try frontennis, more information can be obtained from The U.S. Fronton Athletic Association, The Princeton Club, Box 14, 15 West 43rd Street, New York, N.Y. 10036.

Squash Tennis

As its name suggests, squash tennis is a combination of the two sports. It is played with a tennis racquet (most often, a junior racquet) and tennis ball on a conventional squash court. Primarily a New York City game, squash tennis was once popular among tennis players as a way of keeping in shape during the winter. This was before the advent of indoor tennis, of course. Nowadays, there are few squash tennis players, but the game still has an ardent following in New York City and Washington, D.C.

The scoring and strategy are similar to squash's. The major difference is that the serve must fall in front of the service line. Thus the serve cannot be hard. However, once the ball is in play,

Fig. 53. *The game of squash tennis*

squash tennis is a very lively and very demanding game. The ball tends to carom very rapidly all over the court. Squash tennis is a real power game, rather like that of hard rackets.

As in squash, every point is scored, but unlike squash, the receiver cannot volley the return of serve.

For more information on squash tennis, write National Squash Tennis Association, Yale Club, 50 Vanderbilt Avenue, New York, N.Y. 10017.

Table Tennis

Although many families have a table tennis table in their basement and almost everyone has played the game of "Ping-Pong" at some time in their youth, there are few serious table tennis players in the United States today. There are some 250 table tennis clubs in the United States with about 5,000 serious competitive players. This contrasts sharply with the sport's popularity in Europe and the Far East, where it is a significant participant sport.

The game is played on a table 5 feet by 9 feet, with a 6-inch net in the center. For championship play, the playing area around the "court" must be 46 feet by 26 feet. Championship play is very different from the level seen in most household basements. In top-level play, the players may be many feet away from the table and have to cover as much ground as a racquetball or badminton player. Serious table tennis can be as demanding a sport as any of the racquet sports. However, the U.S. image of the game is generally poor, which has limited its growth as a serious racquet sport.

Racquet and ball control are relatively easy for the beginning player, so table tennis is popular among children. In fact, Bill Price, a former college coach, taught many of his tennis students to play table tennis in the firm belief that they would more easily appreciate the principles of racquet and ball control.

Table tennis is similar in principle to the other net games except that the ball cannot be struck before it bounces—that is to say, it cannot be volleyed. Grips are similar to those of tennis but with one exception, the pen-holder grip often favored by Far Eastern players. Topspin and underspin are vital parts of the advanced player's game, just as they are in tennis.

For more information on table tennis, write U.S. Table Tennis Association, Bridgeton Square Building, Suite 209, St. Louis, Mo. 63044.

Fig. 54. *The game of table tennis*   *Racquet* magazine

Paddle Tennis

The game of paddle tennis is derived directly from tennis. The sport is played on a court 50 feet long by 20 feet wide. The players use a wooden paddle, similar to that used for platform tennis, and a punctured tennis ball. Developed originally as a game for children, paddle tennis flourishes in New York City and southern California. Slightly different games are played on the East and West coasts.

The method of play is similar to regular tennis. However, only one underhand serve is allowed. Otherwise, the play and strategy are those of regular tennis. Doubles lends itself to very aggressive net play, often with all four players at the net slugging the ball at one another. Singles is also an aggressive game, in which the receiver will often follow his return to the net. The server is at a disadvantage in singles with only one serve, and even that one is underhanded.

There are probably no more than 15,000 serious paddle tennis players in the United States, although there may be as many as 8,000 courts. For more information on the sport, write U.S. Paddle Tennis Association, 189 Seeley Street, Brooklyn, N.Y. 11218.

Fig. 55. *The game of paddle tennis*   John Gregory

Fig. 56. *The game of paddleball*

Paddleball

There are three types of paddleball—one-wall, three-wall and four-wall. All the games are derived from handball and have similar courts and rules. The four-wall game is popular in the Midwest but is declining in the face of competition from racquetball. The three-wall game is similar to the four-wall version, but there are few three-wall courts left. The one-wall game is popular in the East, where one-wall handball is most often found. Paddleball was developed by handballers who were looking for an easier game that would not be so rough on their hands.

The four-wall game is played on a court the same size as a racquetball court, but the ceiling is not in play (some courts may be open-air without a ceiling). Strategy is like that of racquetball, but the ball is less bouncy, so around-the-wall balls and Z balls are not played. A major shot is the deep lob to the opponents' backhand. Serve is underarm or sidearm, but the overhead serve is often used in doubles.

The one-wall game is played on a court 20 feet wide (the same width as a racquetball court). The ball is livelier and harder than for the four-wall game. Doubles is the more popular version of the game. Many of the shots are volleys, so the action can be fast and furious. The half volley is also much used. Both four-wall and one-wall games are tough and aggressive, with an emphasis on power.

For more information, write American Paddleball Association, 26 Old Brick Road, New City, N.Y. 10956.

161

Chapter 10

Your Equipment

Choosing the Proper Equipment

As in any sport, to play the game well you'll need the right equipment. In the racquet sports, this means a good racquet (or paddle) that is correctly strung for your level of play, the proper balls in good condition, a properly fitted and comfortable pair of shoes and, generally speaking, clothing that is appropriate to the sport. Then, you will not only have the right equipment to play effectively but also feel confident that you are well prepared, which will help your game psychologically.

In all of our five major racquet sports, selecting the proper equipment is not easy. Nowadays there is tremendous variety in racquet sports equipment in response to the growth of demand in all the sports. Unfortunately, it isn't always possible to get expert advice in stores where racquet sports gear is sold. This is particularly true of stores selling equipment for the less popular racquet sports. So we hope that this chapter will give some idea of the type of equipment that is available in each sport, and we'll try to give you a few general guidelines for the beginning player in each sport.

However, when you decide to buy in an unfamiliar sport, we

Fig. 57. *The racquet sports weapons (from left to right): tennis racquet, platform tennis paddle, badminton racquet, racquetball racquet and squash racquet*

suggest that you seek the advice of a knowledgeable player. In those sports where the teaching professional often sells equipment, as in tennis and squash, you will usually be well advised to seek help in the professional's shop. Although you may pay a little more than in a discount store, the quality of the advice will usually be worth the difference in cost.

Tennis Equipment

As in all our racquet sports, the most significant piece of equipment that you will need is a racquet. In tennis, the choice of racquet and its stringing can make a great deal of difference to your game. A racquet that is too heavy will be difficult for a novice to swing. If the racquet is strung too tightly, you may have problems controlling the ball. So the choice of racquet and stringing is very important.

Until a few years ago, tennis racquets looked pretty much alike. They were almost all made of wood, about 27 inches long, weighed around 13–14 ounces and had similar oval-shaped heads. That they were so similar was largely due to the techniques for making racquets—layers of wood glued together under heat—which had changed little over several decades. However, the rules of tennis do not specify the sizes and shapes of tennis racquets. In fact, you could play tennis with a baseball bat without violating any rule of the game.

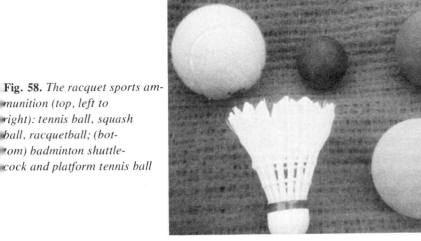

Racquet makers have introduced new materials for racquets, principally steel, aluminum and fiberglass, so that the type and style of racquets now vary widely. The new materials have resulted in racquets that have larger faces than the conventional racquets, are more flexible or stiffer than wood and are often more durable than wood racquets. Thus, the choice of a tennis racquet is more complex nowadays.

Fortunately, wood racquets have by no means been eclipsed by those made from more novel materials. In fact, more than half the tennis racquets sold in the United States are still made from wood. And, of course, wood racquet makers have improved their products in response to the competition.

So we would suggest that if you are a newcomer to tennis, you should start with a good quality wood racquet made by a reputable manufacturer such as Wilson, Dunlop, Davis or Bancroft (there are others equally good). It should be of medium weight (around 13½ ounces strung, for men, a little lighter for a woman or a youngster). If you buy the racquet unstrung, as are most quality racquets, you should have it strung with a top-quality nylon at around 55 pounds of tension. Your racquet, strung with nylon, should cost no more than $50.

Later, as your game improves, you can experiment with the better metal or fiberglass racquets; your local pro shop will often have demonstrator racquets that you can borrow for a day or two. You can also experiment with different string tensions— tighter if you are a hard hitter, less tight if you are a more con-

165

trolled player. You might also wish to try gut strings, which are generally more responsive than nylon but are more expensive and not so durable. Gut is often easier on your arm. Most good players prefer gut and consider the extra expense and more frequent need to restring to be worthwhile.

In contrast to racquets, tennis balls are quite closely specified by the U.S. Tennis Association. Thus, you should buy and use only tennis balls that are approved by the USTA. You will discover, however, that all tennis balls are not quite alike. Some will appear marginally heavier than others, some will last longer, some will fly faster through the air, and so on. It's largely a matter of finding a brand that suits your game or the playing conditions. You'll be able to judge that better as your game improves.

How long a can of three balls will last is largely a matter of how you play and the surface on which you play. However, a can of balls costs only $2–$3, so it's a good idea to open a fresh one every time you play a match and to keep the used balls for your practice sessions. Incidentally, a bucket of used balls can come in very handy if you wish to practice your serve alone on the court. So don't throw away your old balls.

Tennis shoes will be an important purchase. Your feet have to put up with a lot of punishment on the tennis court, so you should devote some time and effort to selecting the right shoes. As with racquets, the design of tennis shoes has changed considerably over the past few years. Tennis shoes are no longer the flimsy canvas sneakers that could be purchased for a couple of dollars at a dime store. A good pair of shoes from a reputable maker can cost over $30.

The soles of tennis shoes may be rubber or polyurethane, a synthetic material. Rubber generally offers more traction but wears faster. The uppers of tennis shoes may be a high-quality canvas or leather. Leather shoes will last longer than canvas but may not fit an unusually shaped foot so easily. Also, the soles of a leather shoe may wear out before the uppers. The choice is up to you and your pocketbook.

However, do look for a shoe that is well padded around the

heel and instep. Make sure that the inside of the shoe is smooth, with no exposed or rough stitching, and that there is plenty of room inside for your toes. Get your shoes fitted in a sporting goods store that has experienced fitters. And wear a pair of good quality socks or even two pairs for extra comfort.

Tennis clothing, too, has come a long way from the all-white outfits that used to be de rigueur in the tennis clubs in the first half of the century. Now, tennis clothes come in a wide variety of styles and colors to suit almost every personal whim. The choice is largely up to you. Remember to select clothes that will let you move easily and will absorb perspiration well. Cotton is usually more comfortable. Your clothes should also wash and dry quickly.

Men will need shirts and shorts. Women can wear dresses or shorts and a blouse. Headband and wristbands to absorb sweat are useful, especially when playing outdoors in warm weather. In colder climes or to wear after play, a warm-up suit is valuable. How much you spend on these items is up to you. However, you should be quite sure that you wish to continue with the sport before you invest a lot of money in equipment. Fortunately, much tennis wear is usable in our other racquet sports, so the investment may not be a total loss should you decide that tennis is not for you.

Platform Tennis Equipment

The selection of a paddle for platform tennis play is not quite so complicated as the choice of a tennis racquet, but if you should continue with your play, a good paddle will be worth the time and money involved in its selection. Unlike tennis, in platform tennis the paddle is closely specified in the rules of the American Platform Tennis Association, so the choice is somewhat simplified.

Paddles are 17 inches long with an oval face that is 8¼ inches wide. Traditionally, paddles are made from a hard wood, but aluminum alloy and fiberglass racquets have recently become available. Not all are approved by the APTA, however, so check before you buy.

The face is perforated with up to 87 holes to reduce air resistance as the racquet is swung and to help grip the ball. The newer metal and fiberglass paddles often have fewer holes. The fiberglass racquets are more resilient and grip the ball better.

The paddle has to be swung quickly, so it's important to pick a racquet that you can swing easily. You'll find a greater variation in weight than with tennis racquets—from 13 to 18 ounces. A novice player will probably find a lighter racquet easier to swing and less tiring on the arm muscles. Almost all advanced players use heavier paddles to overcome the momentum of the heavy sponge rubber ball.

As for tennis, we suggest that the novice buy a traditional wood paddle from a reputable maker, such as Marcraft or Vittert. You should usually choose a grip that is about one size smaller than your tennis grip, although the fiberglass racquets, such as those made by Paddle Pro, have sizes that compare with tennis racquets. Expert advice from a good player will be of considerable help in choosing your first paddle. Unlike the implements in our other racquet sports, the paddle is solid and does not require stringing. A well-made paddle should last you for many seasons of play, so it's important to pick the best one right away. A top-quality paddle will cost you about $45.

The platform tennis ball is of solid sponge rubber with a fuzzy nylon coating that is colored orange or yellow. The balls are closely specified by the APTA, so you should buy only balls that have been approved by them. The nylon cover wears off quickly in play, since the court surface is very abrasive, so you should use new balls every time you go out to play. Platform tennis balls retail for approximately $1.20 each.

Clothing for platform play is very informal except in the better tournaments. You may wish to wear shorts and a shirt with a warm-up suit on cold days. However, most players prefer an old pair of pants and as many sweaters as the temperature and personal preference seem to dictate. In fact, there almost appears to be a cult of genteel scruffiness among club platform tennis players. In other words, almost anything goes as long as you are comfortable on the court. Remember, too, that the platform court is quite small, so you may run into the screens occasionally. When that happens, it's a good idea to be well protected with clothes that can take rough treatment.

Despite the informality in clothing, you should wear a good pair of tennis shoes on the platform court. The surface of a platform court is painted with an abrasive material to assist the traction of the players. This surface is very tough on shoes, so a cheap pair of tennis shoes will wear out very quickly while not protecting your feet. Look for tennis shoes with polyurethane soles, which will wear longer than the softer rubber soles. The shoes should be well padded around the heel and instep. Many platform players favor canvas uppers for comfort, but leather tennis shoes are fine, too.

Gloves may be a necessity if you play in the colder parts of the country in the winter months. Leather gloves are best for keeping a firm grip on the paddle. Some players cut a hole in a wool sock, which can then go over the handle and the arm and wrist in one go. That allows the player to keep his hand warm and keep a firm grip at the same time. Similarly, some form of headgear is advisable in cold weather.

Badminton Equipment

If you have played tennis or squash, you will find that the badminton racquet is a very delicate instrument indeed. Although similar in length to a squash or tennis racquet, the typical badminton racquet weighs a mere 5 ounces or less and, if used improperly, can be quite fragile. So it's important to choose your badminton racquet with some care if you are to get the best from it and have it last a long time.

Badminton racquets are not specified by the rules of the International Badminton Federation but, unlike tennis racquets, are all basically the same shape. At one time, racquet frames were made entirely from wood, but nowadays the shafts are usually aluminum, steel or graphite and the heads wood or aluminum. Steel and graphite shafts are much stronger than wood and can be designed to give almost any degree of flex. Many badminton racquets are sold already strung with nylon but gut is preferred for tournament play.

If you are a newcomer to badminton, we suggest you buy a good quality racquet with a wood head and a metal shaft from a maker such as Yonex or Wilson. It should be strung with nylon at about 13 pounds of tension. Such a racquet should cost you no more than $35. Later you may decide to have your racquet strung with gut or to test an all-metal racquet. However, as a beginner you will do best with a medium-flex racquet weighing around 4½ ounces.

Your grip size will be smaller than for tennis because of the need for wrist snap; make sure that the last three fingers of your hand almost touch your palm when wrapped around the handle in your normal manner of gripping. The usual range of grips is 3¼ to 3½ inches.

Perhaps more than in any of our other racquet sports, the choice of the shuttlecock can be critical to your play. The badminton shuttlecock is also a very fragile device and is easily damaged. If you use the wrong type of bird you will damage it quickly. It is possible to use up several shuttlecocks during one evening's play.

The traditional badminton shuttlecock has from 14 to 16 feathers fixed in a cork base about an inch in diameter. Since the feathers will perform differently according to the temperature and humidity of the day, there are 15 different weights of birds. The weight is determined by a piece of metal set within the cork base and may vary between one fifth and one sixth of an ounce. The shape of the feathers will also affect the speed of the bird. The specifications for a shuttlecock are laid down by the rules of the IBF.

According to the rules of play, the correct weight of shuttlecock for a given day is determined by hitting the bird with a full underhand swing from one backline to the other. It should fall between 1 foot and 2 feet 6 inches short of the opposing backline. That's a tough test for most novice players. By all means use the test, but if you have any doubt, opt for the shuttle that flies faster. Slower shuttlecocks slow down the play, which then becomes largely defensive and increases the possibility of early damage to the bird. Faster shuttles will lead to a higher quality of play with a wider variety of shots.

Feather shuttlecocks cost around $12 per dozen. A cheaper alternative is a plastic shuttlecock, which retails for approximately $8 per dozen. Plastic birds are accepted by most clubs today and are used in some tournaments. Novice players will find the plastic birds last longer and give more consistent play. They are also available in different speeds and weights.

Some conservative badminton clubs still insist on all-white clothing for their members, but, in general, tennis clothing is very suitable for badminton play. As in tennis, the clothes should be loose enough to permit free movement, especially for the overhead strokes that are so vital in badminton play. A warm-up suit is useful to prevent cooling off between matches or when starting play.

A good pair of tennis shoes is essential for badminton. Some clubs have synthetic carpet courts that provide excellent traction, but many clubs play on polished wood floors which can be slippery. If the latter is the case with your club, look for tennis shoes that have softer rubber soles. Such shoes will give you excellent traction on wood floors. Badminton is a game of quick stops and starts, so the shoes must fit well and be adequately padded to prevent blisters. Since badminton is played competitively indoors, leather shoes are not really necessary but will do no harm to the court or the wearer.

Squash Equipment

In squash, the racquets, balls and clothing are all specified by the rules, although the U.S. Squash Racquets Association has made some important changes in the past few years with respect to the ball and may be expected to make more as the popularity of squash grows.

According to the USSRA, the racquet head has to be made of wood, must be no more than 27 inches long and have a circular head that is no more than 9 inches wide. Racquets for the 70+ ball weigh 7½ to 9 ounces strung.

As in tennis, you will be better off going to your local pro for your first racquet or, if your club does not have a professional, getting some advice from a better player. However, since you will be using the new 70+ ball, we suggest that you look for a racquet that is evenly balanced and weighs 8 ounces or less. It should be a medium-flex racquet and swing easily in your hand. Squash racquets are available in only one grip size, but the shape of the handle may vary. Reputable U.S. makers include Bancroft, Wilson and Cragin. A good squash racquet should cost you about $40 strung. However, it's not worth spending a lot of money on a first racquet, since a beginner is likely to damage it by hitting the walls or the floor.

The best racquets are sold unstrung. Have yours strung with nylon at about 30 pounds of tension. Better players favor gut, but the difference in playability is not noticeable by the novice player, and gut will wear out faster than nylon.

The 70+ squash ball is made of hard green rubber and comes in fast (winter) and slow (summer) varieties. The balls cost $3 each but will last for a season. In response to popular demand, the 70+ ball was approved by the USSRA because it is easier for beginners and less powerful players to use. In fact, the 70+ ball may be a major factor in helping new players to get started in playing squash and to stay with the sport. The old ball was too hard and fast for the beginner to rally properly, which led to an early feeling of frustration. The new ball helps get around that problem.

The rules of the USSRA require that players wear all-white or solid pastel clothing. The argument is that this makes the squash ball easier to see, an important consideration in the fast pace of squash play. However, in casual club play, the rules seem to be bent considerably. It seems likely the association will modify its rules to permit most types of tennis clothing.

As in the other racquet sports, the cardinal rule is to choose clothes that give unrestricted movement of the arms and legs. However, squash clothing should also be chosen for its absorbent qualities, since the players will sweat considerably even in the colder months. Moisture on the court can be dangerous for a player's footing and should be prevented or at least toweled off when it happens.

Well-fitted tennis shoes with good traction are a must for squash play. Some squash courts have quite slippery floors, so the rubber-soled deck-gripping type of tennis shoe is best suited to squash. Canvas shoes are quite adequate but some players prefer leather tennis shoes. As in the other racquet sports, proper padding around the heel and instep is essential. Blisters can be a problem in squash, so proper fitting and well-made shoes are a must.

Wristbands and headbands are very useful in squash if you have a tendency to sweat profusely. A small towel tucked into your shorts may come in handy. If your grip becomes slick from sweat, you may prefer to regrip your racquet with toweling, which will be much more absorbent than the normal leather grip, or you can wear a thin leather glove.

Racquetball Equipment

One of the more appealing advantages of racquetball for the newcomer to the sport is that it is perhaps the least expensive of our five sports in terms of equipment. Strung racquets cost under

$30 generally, there are no requirements for special clothing, and the balls are quite cheap. You will need a pair of tennis shoes, of course, but most likely you'll have those from whatever other racquet sport you've played.

The racquets and balls used in the sport are closely specified by the rules of the two national associations—the U.S. Racquetball Association and the International Racquetball Association. The specifications say that the total length and width of a racquet must not exceed 27 inches. In practice, this means that the racquets are usually less than 18 inches long and no more than 9 inches wide. There are no restrictions as to material for the frame and the handle, but the racquet must have a thong which is wrapped around the player's wrist during play to prevent the racquet from flying out of his hand.

Early racquets were made from wood, but now only a few cheap imports use wood (and should be avoided, since they are of poor quality). Currently, racquets are made from either aluminum alloy or fiberglass. Some recently introduced models use a composite of fiberglass and aluminum much like certain types of tennis racquets. The metal racquets are strong and give more power in the hands of a hard hitter. The fiberglass racquets are more flexible and produce more control for a skilled player but are often prone to breakage either in play or when the player hits the wall accidentally.

The head designs of racquets vary from oval to almost square. The selection seems to be a matter of personal preference. Grips are sometimes rubber, which will last longer than leather and is easier to clean. That's important, since racquets often get slick from the oils in the hand that are produced when a player perspires. Virtually all racquetball racquets are sold strung with nylon at around 25 to 30 pounds of tension. Gut does not appear to offer any special advantage to the racquetballer.

For the novice we suggest that you buy a metal racquet that is evenly balanced and weighs around 9 ounces strung. Your grip size should be smaller than for tennis, so that your fingers are almost touching the palm of your hand when you grip the racquet correctly. The leading makers, specializing in racquetball racquets, are Leach and Ektelon, but many top tennis racquet makers are now offering racquetball racquets, too. It's best to buy from the pro shop if your club has one, or to get some advice from a more experienced player.

Many racquetballers prefer to play with a glove on the racquet hand to help absorb some of the abundant perspiration and to assist the grip. Some players favor a full glove, others the half glove which has the fingers uncovered. If you have difficulty in holding the racquet (and you are sure that the grip size is right for you), try a glove or half glove. You'll find wristbands and headbands useful, too, in absorbing sweat.

Dress on the racquetball court has always been very casual, although there are now clothes designed specifically for the sport. For both men and women, loose-fitting T-shirts and running-type shorts often seem to be the rule, but tennis clothes are becoming more popular as the sport attracts a wider range of players. The two national associations are actively campaigning to raise the standard of both dress and deportment on the racquetball court. Efforts in both areas are sorely needed in some clubs and are to be welcomed.

You will also find many racquetballers wearing eye guards on the court, since there have been some serious eye injuries from both the ball and errant racquets. The newer eye guards are quite comfortable to wear and restrict vision very little. They are available also for players who normally wear eyeglasses to play. They are essential for such players and very sensible for those who do not need eyeglasses.

The racquetball is a pressurized rubber ball, a little smaller than a tennis ball and not covered with fabric. It is rather more bouncy than a tennis ball; the degree of bounce is specified by the rules of the sport. Until recently, the makers had difficulty producing balls that were consistent, so that two balls from the same pressurized can could bounce and perform quite differently. This situation is improving, but the balls still need better quality control. A ball may last for less than one match or for several matches. As in tennis, it's best to buy new balls whenever you go out to play seriously. A can of two balls will cost $3. Used balls are good for practice, however.

Chapter 11

Conditioning for the Racquet Sports

Playing Is Not Enough

Many Americans have turned to the racquet sports as a pleasant way of getting exercise and keeping fit. While it is certainly true that the racquet sports do provide exercise, none of them will give you enough exercise to become fit and stay that way unless you play every day. For example, most professional tennis players claim that the best conditioning for tennis is to play the sport. However, the pros play every day, either in competition or in practice; but when they stop playing, they immediately take up some other exercise program to maintain their level of fitness. So the racquet sports player who plays once or twice a week cannot expect to improve his general fitness level nor to be at peak fitness for his particular sport without a conditioning program.

There are three different requirements for playing any of the racquet sports. They are (1) stamina, the ability to play intensively for a long period of time; (2) flexibility, the ability of muscles to stretch to accommodate the rapid movements of each sport; and (3) muscular strength, the ability to perform the strokes and footwork for each sport. Each of our racquet sports will help these qualities, but they will not maintain them unless you play intensively almost every day.

We are not going to give you a complete exercise program for each of our five major racquet sports. That is not the function of this book. Instead, we will indicate in general and in particular the conditioning you will need for each of our sports and tell you the benefits to be derived in terms of fitness from each of the sports. You will then be able to get an idea of the conditioning program that will be right for you based on your particular sport and the extent of your participation.

If you do not already have an exercise program that you are following, we suggest that you get one of the many excellent books now available on conditioning. We have found *The West Point Fitness and Diet Book,* by Colonel James L. Anderson and Martin Cohen (Rawson Associates, New York) to be excellent in all respects. The book gives programs for general fitness, for flexibility and for specific sports. The authors list ten lifetime sports that promote overall physical fitness. Interestingly, racquetball is fourth on the list, squash is fifth, tennis ninth, and badminton tenth. We would argue that badminton deserves a higher ranking, but in general we agree with Anderson and Cohen. Their top ranking goes to bicycling, incidentally.

One caution is in order before we continue. If you are over 35, or have a history of physical problems, or have been relatively inactive for several years, we recommend that you seek the advice of your physician before either taking up one of the racquet sports or embarking on a conditioning program for a specific sport. Most of our racquet sports can be vigorous and demanding, particularly on the heart and lungs. If you have any doubt at all about your ability to play, talk to your doctor. He will be able to advise you on how to proceed. It is extremely unlikely that you will be advised not to play one of our five sports—they are all lifetime sports when played properly—but they should be approached with some care, since they all have some risk attached.

Building Your Stamina

As you might suppose, the sports that take the most out of you will do the most for building your stamina. Thus, platform tennis, which is played only in the doubles version, does not require much stamina and will do little for increasing it. On the other hand, squash, which is usually played as singles and has lengthy rallies and points with little time for recovery, does call for stamina and, if played regularly, will build your endurance.

So, your exercise program should be aimed at developing the capacity of your heart and lungs to withstand prolonged physical effort. This is best achieved with a daily routine that involves running, swimming or bicycling for significant distances. The appropriate distances will vary according to your age and general conditioning, but the usual objective is to raise your heart rate to about 60 percent of its maximum for 30 minutes or so. The West Point book gives you the details on checking yourself out for this and other levels of cardiorespiratory fitness. Remember that this level is something that you will have to work up to over a long period of time.

Unless you are a very competent singles player, tennis will do little for your heart and lungs. There are so many pauses and rest periods in tennis, especially in doubles, that your heart will rarely sustain a high rate for very long. On a hot day, of course, the heart and lungs will have to work harder, so tennis can be physically tiring.

Both racquetball and squash can have much more of a conditioning effect than tennis and platform tennis. As a squash or racquetball novice, the points may not last long enough for you to sustain a high heart rate for an effective period of time, but as your game improves you will find more demands being placed on your heart and lungs. Nonetheless, you should still have a regular running or bicycling program when you take up squash or racquetball. Of course, on the days when you play, you will not also require the running or bicycling. In fact, to do both in the same day might overtax you physically instead of giving you the feeling of exhilaration that normally comes from the proper amount of physical activity.

Badminton is somewhat similar to squash and racquetball in its conditioning effect. The game can be very demanding on the heart and lungs for the better player. Naturally, the better the player, the greater the conditioning effect. However, we have to make a distinction between doubles and singles. Except for the very top players, badminton doubles will not improve your cardiorespiratory system, whereas singles can have quite an effect. The singles game requires a lot of court coverage with many fast changes of direction and fewer pauses than in tennis. Singles rallies can be quite long between two good players of similar ability. So for badminton singles, you will need a running or bicycling program only on the days when you do not play.

Improving Your Flexibility

All our five major racquet sports require significant muscular flexibility. It is characteristic of each of the sports that you will have to stretch your arm and leg muscles in particular to get to the ball and to make some of the strokes. If you are not sufficiently flexible, you will run the risk of pulling or tearing a muscle. While a muscle that has been pulled will recover (given enough rest), a torn muscle may be sufficiently serious to require surgical repair and a long period of abstinence from your racquet sport. So it's very important to devote time to flexibility exercises —the more so as you get older and the muscles themselves age.

Your regular program should contain exercises for general body flexibility—again, we would suggest the exercises detailed in the West Point book. However, you should also have a number of exercises to perform just before you go out onto the court, so that you warm up the specific muscles you will be using out there.

Proper warm-up will reduce the chances of damaging a muscle by overexertion during the early play. Five minutes is all that is required. Getting to the court five minutes early may save you many hours of recovery from a damaged muscle. It's worth the investment in time.

You can also build flexibility off the court and outside your regular conditioning program by stretching and flexing your muscles as you sit at your desk or while driving a car or working around the house. Don't overlook the opportunities for exercise that occur all day and every day.

Speeding Up Your Footwork

You will almost certainly find when you begin a new racquet sport that you seem inordinately slow in getting around the court. This will be partly due to your undeveloped reflexes for the sport and partly due to poor footwork. In all our sports, an improvement in your footwork will bring about a drastic rise in the level of your game.

So how do you speed up your footwork? Simple running might strengthen your leg muscles but will do little for your quickness around the court. The distances you have to run on a squash or tennis court are too short for normal running training to have much effect (although, of course, running will improve your cardiorespiratory system, as we noted earlier). There are two specific activities you can try to speed up your footwork.

First, to make you lighter on your feet, we suggest you skip rope regularly. You will have noticed that boxers, who are also constrained to move quickly in a confined area, devote a lot of time to skipping rope. Not only will rope jumping make you lighter on your toes, but it will also build your leg muscles and, if you keep it up for long enough, improve your heart and lung capacity. A few minutes a day with the jump rope is all that's needed to improve your footwork. In fact, when you begin you may have trouble jumping rope for as long as one minute. Keep trying and you'll soon see some results on the court. For best results, use a leather jumprope with ball-bearing handles.

Second, practice running with lots of starts and stops around the court where you play. Henry Hines, the former track star who is now a tennis coach, advises a routine of running around tennis balls placed in a slalom-like course on the lines of a court. You can devise similar routines for running within any of the courts. Only a couple of minutes at a time is required, but you must have the feeling that you are pushing yourself.

Strengthening Your Muscles

All our major racquet sports can help in strengthening your muscles, particularly in the stomach and lower body. Unfortunately, only one side of the body is used for hitting the ball, so the arm and shoulder muscles do not receive the same benefit on both sides of the body. This can be seen in the extreme on Australian Rod Laver, whose left arm is much bigger (and even an inch or two longer) than his right. There's not much danger of that happening to the casual racquet sports player, of course.

However, you may notice that your wrist muscles become much stronger on your racquet arm. If that's a concern to you, try squeezing an old tennis ball in your other hand from time to time. Or you can train with light weights in both hands to improve the strength of your arm and wrist muscles on either side.

The racquet sports vary in their effect on your lower body. Many players feel that badminton is the ultimate in terms of strengthening the leg muscles because the game calls for so many rapid movements. However, squash also has some violent movements around the court with long rallies that tend to punish the leg muscles and joints. Squash does not have quite the beneficial effect on the muscles of the more graceful badminton footwork.

Racquetball also has some rapid movements around the court but without the violent stops and starts of squash. This is because the bouncier racquetball ball gives the player more time to get to it and execute the stroke. Thus racquetball is an excellent conditioner for the leg muscles.

Tennis singles will help your legs if you play often enough and have some long matches. Although the distances covered on a tennis court are potentially greater than in our other racquet sports, most tennis players do not have to cover all the court unless they are playing against a very skilled opponent. And, as we noted earlier, tennis has frequent pauses in the action, which allow the muscles to recover quickly.

Platform tennis will not do much for your leg muscles, since there is little movement other than quick, boxerlike steps to get to the ball. Rope jumping will help your platform tennis, but it's doubtful if platform play will do much to strengthen your leg muscles unless you play every day for several hours. It's unlikely that you'd have the time for that much platform tennis.

A Few Words on Injuries

Proper conditioning will much reduce the chance of an injury from playing the racquet sports. However, injury is always a possibility no matter how fit you are or how good a player. If you are injured on court, stop playing and get first aid or proper medical treatment right away. Although professional players will, unwisely, continue after injury, there is no reason for the amateur to do so. Stopping after injury will get you back into play faster than continuing and making the injury more serious.

Chapter 12

Competing in Your Racquet Sport

The Essence of Racquet Sports Play

As we noted in the opening chapter, the racquet sports resemble gladiatorial combat in that they pit one player against another (or two pairs of players). This aspect of the racquet sports quite obviously has significant appeal for most players. There is a very definite desire to win—to beat the opponent—among virtually all racquet sports players. Thus, it seems appropriate to conclude this book with a chapter on finding more competition in each of the sports that we have examined.

This chapter will tell you what to expect in the way of competition in our sports and show you how to go about getting more competition for yourself. Obviously we cannot cover every tournament and league in detail, but we can show you where to get started and where to go for help in getting more information.

Remember, though, that most of the organizations in the racquet sports are still run by volunteers. Even where the sport is sufficiently large to justify a national office and an executive director, much of the grass-roots activity is volunteer organized. Volunteers are happy to help newcomers to their sport but may be overworked and, often, more than a little harassed. If you have problems in seeking out competition, keep trying—you will eventually find that every racquet sport has more than enough competitive activity to satisfy every level of player.

How to Compete in Tennis

Along with the boom in tennis has come a profusion of tournaments and other competitions at all levels from the national to the intraclub. Your problem is knowing where to start.

At the local level, many towns have municipal tennis courts, and some organize tournaments for residents. Often the only entry fee is a can of balls or some equally small dollar amount. If you play at an indoor tennis club, you may find that the club has regular round-robin tournaments for all grades of players. If you are a member of a country club or tennis club, chances are that your club has its own club tournaments for several classes of player in both singles and doubles. Your club may also have a ladder where you can arrange individual challenge matches and so move up the ladder (or down if you are beaten). When you first start playing tennis, you should look for these local events to start out on competitive play.

As you improve, you may wish to play in a citywide or even a statewide tournament. At this stage, you should join the U.S. Tennis Association, which sanctions many tournaments around the country. You will not be able to play in a sanctioned tournament unless you join the USTA. To join, write USTA, 51 East 42nd Street, New York, N.Y. 10017. Membership costs, $25 for a family, $13 for an individual and $6 for a junior (under 18). The USTA will give you the name and address of your local sectional office where you can get tournament schedules for your part of the country.

How to Compete in Platform Tennis

As you might expect, the arrangements for competing in platform tennis are very similar to those in regular tennis. However, most platform tennis is played in country clubs or tennis clubs where organized competition is a vital part of the club. There are a few commercial platform tennis centers that operate in much the same way as a commercial indoor tennis club and often offer the same type of leagues and round-robin competitions.

So if you wish to compete in platform tennis, you should join a country club or tennis club with platform courts. Some clubs have special memberships for those people who wish only to play platform tennis during the winter months. Many clubs welcome such members, since they increase the usage of the club in the normally slow winter months. Not only do most clubs organize internal tournaments but they also have team play against neighboring clubs. Interclub play can be very exciting and not out of reach of the relative newcomer to the sport. Since platform tennis is a very social game, the standard of play is not necessarily high at the interclub level.

Just as the USTA sanctions state and regional tennis tournaments, the American Platform Tennis Association sanctions a wide variety of platform tennis tournaments. To play in a sanctioned tournament you must be a member of the APTA. To join, write APTA, 52 Upper Montclair Plaza, Upper Montclair, N.J. 07043. Family membership costs $20 per year, individual membership $10 and junior membership $5.

How to Compete in Racquetball

Since racquetball is a relatively new sport, there is less organized competition than in our other sports. However, the situation is changing very rapidly owing to demand and the activities of the two national racquetball associations. In parts of the country where racquetball has become well entrenched, principally California and the Midwest, there is much competitive activity in the sport.

Racquetball is played in YMCAs and in commercial clubs. The latter are spreading very rapidly to all parts of the country. Such clubs often organize informal competitions as a way of promoting themselves to new members. They also organize ladders and round-robin tournaments for established members. There appears to be little interclub racquetball at present, but that situation may change very shortly.

State and regional tournaments for amateurs are organized by the two competing national associations—the U.S. Racquetball Association and the International Racquetball Association. To join the USRA (membership $12 per year) write USRA, 4101 Dempster, Skokie, Ill. 60076. To join the IRA (membership $12 per year) write IRA, 5545 Murray Avenue, Suite 202, Memphis, Tenn. 38117. Confusingly, both associations claim to be the leading group, but the USRA appears to be better financed and more likely to be successful in the long run. We can only hope that the two organizations will get together in the near future for the benefit of racquetball and racquetballers.

How to Compete in Badminton

Despite a much lower profile than our other racquet sports, there is a great deal of competitive badminton played in the United States. Although there are few clubs where badminton is played to the exclusion of other racquet sports, much badminton is played in private athletic or sports clubs in the larger towns and cities. In smaller towns, badminton clubs may meet several nights a week in local college or high school gymnasiums.

Badminton is quite a social game, so much competition is played in the form of mixed doubles. Clubs organize their own tournaments for all classes of members, and interclub competitions are common. Once you have found your local badminton club, you should have no difficulty in finding suitable competition. If you have trouble locating a club, write U.S. Badminton Association, Box 237, Swartz Creek, Mich. 48473.

As in our other racquet sports, the USBA sanctions many regional and state badminton tournaments across the country. For your membership fee of $20 per year you will receive tournament schedules and addresses of local badminton associations. The local groups can tell you about tournaments in your area.

As of this writing, there is no professional play in badminton, unlike our other racquet sports, although professional badminton has been approved by the International Badminton Federation. World-class badminton is rarely seen in the United States, although we have some players of international standard. We can only hope that this situation will soon be remedied.

How to Compete in Squash

Activity in squash is largely concentrated in the bigger cities and university towns, particularly in the Northeast. Much squash is played in private university and athletic clubs that often have some restrictions on membership. Fortunately, the increasing popularity of squash in the past few years has led to the opening of a number of commercial squash clubs whose courts are open to all who can pay the hourly fee. It seems likely that the trend toward commercial clubs will continue.

However, most of the competitive activity in squash is based around the older private clubs. To play in tournaments where you are not a club member, you must join the U.S. Squash Racquets Association or one of the regional associations affiliated with the USSRA. For details on membership, write USSRA, 211 Ford Road, Bala Cynwyd, Pa. 19004. Until recently, there were separate national associations for men and women, but the two have now merged—a welcome move.

The USSRA can supply a list of tournaments and the names and addresses of the directors of the various regional associations. Membership in the association costs $15 per year for adults and $5 for those under 21.

A Racquet Sports Bibliography

A book such as this cannot hope to answer all your questions about the racquet sports, so we'd like to give you a short list of some of the books that we've found useful for racquet sports players.

Badminton

Badminton, by E. Brown. Transatlantic Arts, Levittown, N.Y., 1975.
Sports Illustrated Badminton, by J.F. Devlin with Rex Lardner. Lippincott, New York, 1967.
Winning Badminton, by K.R. Davidson and L.R. Gustavson. Ronald Press, New York, 1964.

Platform Tennis

How to Play Platform Tennis, by Dick Squires. McGraw-Hill, New York, 1977.
The Complete Book of Platform Tennis, by Dick Squires. Houghton-Mifflin, Boston, 1974.
Platform Tennis, by Bob Callaway and Richard Hughes. Lippincott, New York, 1977.

Racquetball

Off the Wall, by Charles Brumfield and Jeffrey Bairstow. The Dial Press, New York, 1978.
The Racquetball Book, by Steve Strandemo with Bill Bruns. Pocket Books, New York, 1977.
Inside Racquetball, by Charles Leve. Contemporary Books, Chicago, 1973.

Squash

The Book of Squash, by Peter Wood. Little, Brown, Boston, 1972.

Smart Squash, by Austin Francis. Lippincott, New York, 1977.

Contemporary Squash, by Al Molloy, Jr. Contemporary Books, Chicago, 1978.

Tennis

Tennis for the Future, by Vic Braden with Bill Bruns. Little, Brown, Boston, 1978.

Tennis: How to Play, How to Win, by the editors of Tennis Magazine. Simon & Schuster, New York, 1979.

The Game of Doubles in Tennis, by William F. Talbert and Bruce S. Old. Lippincott, New York, 1956.

General

Enjoying Racquet Sports, by the Diagram Group. Paddington Press, New York, 1978.

The Other Racquet Sports, by Dick Squires. McGraw-Hill, New York, 1978.

Conditioning

The West Point Fitness and Diet Book, by Col. J.L. Anderson and M. Cohen. Rawson Associates, New York, 1977.

Appendix

The Rules of the Racquet Sports

The following rules have been abridged slightly and are the playing rules of each of our five major racquet sports. We have omitted those rules relating to tournament play and specifications for courts and equipment. Complete rules can be obtained from the secretary of each national association (addresses given at the end of each set of rules).

THE RULES OF BADMINTON

Rule 5. Players.

(a) The word "Player" applies to all those taking part in a game.

(b) The game shall be played, in the case of the doubles game, by two players a side, and in the case of the singles game, by one player a side.

(c) The side for the time being having the right to serve shall be called the "In" side, and the opposing side shall be called the "Out" side.

Rule 6. The Toss. Before commencing play the opposing sides shall toss, and the side winning the toss shall have the option of—

(a) Serving first; or (b) Not serving first; or (c) Choosing ends.

The side losing the toss shall then have choice of any alternative remaining.

Rule 7. Scoring.

(a) The doubles and men's singles game consists of 15 or 21 points, as may be arranged. Provided that in a game of 15 points, when the score is 13-all, the side which first reached 13 has the option of "Setting" the game to 5, and that when the score is 14-all, the side which first reached 14 has the option of "Setting" the game to 3. After the game has been "Set" the score is called "Love All," and the side which first scores 5 or 3 points, according as the game has been "Set" at 13- or 14-all, wins the game. In either case the claim to "Set" the game must be made before the next service is delivered after the score has reached 13-all or 14-all. Provided also that in a game of 21 points the same method of scoring be adopted, substituting 19 and 20 for 13 and 14.

(b) The ladies' singles game consists of 11 points. Provided that when the score is "9-all" the player who first reached 9 has the option of "Setting" the game to 3, and when the score is "10-all" the player who first reached 10 has the option of "Setting" the game to 2.

(c) A side rejecting the option of "Setting" at the first opportunity shall not be thereby barred from "Setting" if a second opportunity arises.

(d) In handicap games "Setting" is not permitted.

Rule 8. The opposing sides shall contest the best of three games, unless otherwise agreed. The players shall change ends at the commencement of the second game and also of the third game (if any). In the third game the players shall change ends when the leading score reaches—

(a) 8 in a game of 15 points;

(b) 6 in a game of 11 points;

(c) 11 in a game of 21 points;

or, in handicap events, when one of the sides has scored half the total number of points required to win the game (the next highest numbers being taken in case of fractions). When it has been agreed to play only one game the players shall change ends as provided above for the third game.

If, inadvertently, the players omit to change ends as provided in this Rule at the score indicated, the ends shall be changed immediately the mistake is discovered, and the existing score shall stand.

Doubles Play

Rule 9.

(a) It having been decided which side is to have the first service, the player in the right-hand service court of that side commences the game by serving to the player in the service court diagonally opposite. If the latter player returns the shuttle before it touches the ground it is to be returned by one of the "In" side, and then returned by one of the "Out" side, and so on, until a fault is made or the shuttle ceases to be "In Play." (*Vide* paragraph (b).) If a fault is made by the "In" side, its right to continue serving is lost, as only one player on the side beginning a game is entitled to do so (*vide* Rule 11), and the opponent in the right-hand service court then becomes the server; but if the service is not returned, or the fault is made by the "Out" side, the "In" side scores a point. The "In" side players then change from one service court to the other, the service now being from the left-hand service court to the player in the service court diagonally opposite. So long as a side remains "In," service is delivered alternately from each service court into the one diagonally opposite, the change being made by the "In" side when, and only when, a point is added to its score.

(b) The first service of a side in each inning shall be made from the right-hand service court. A "Service" is delivered as soon as the shuttle is struck by the server's racket. The shuttle is thereafter "In Play" until it touches the ground, or until a fault or "Let" occurs, or except as provided in Rule 19. After the service is delivered, the server and the player served to may take up any position they choose on their side of the net, irrespective of any boundary lines.

Rule 10. The player served to may alone receive the service, but should the shuttle touch, or be struck by, his partner the "In" side scores a point. No player may receive two consecutive services in the same game, except as provided in Rule 12.

Rule 11. Only one player of the side beginning a game shall be entitled to serve in its first innings. In all subsequent innings each partner shall have the right and they shall serve consecutively. The side winning a game shall always serve first in the next game, but either of the winners may serve and either of the losers may receive the service.

Rule 12. If a player serves out of turn, or from the wrong service court (owing to a mistake as to the service court from which service is at the time being in order), *and his side wins the rally,* it shall be a "Let," provided that such "Let" be claimed and allowed, or ordered by the umpire before the next succeeding service is delivered.

If a player of the "Out" side standing in the wrong service court is prepared to receive the service when it is delivered, *and his side wins the rally,* it shall be a "Let," provided that such "Let" be claimed and allowed, or ordered by the umpire, before the next succeeding service is delivered.

If in either of the above cases the side at fault *loses the rally*, the mistake shall stand and the players' positions shall not be corrected.

Should a player inadvertently change sides when he should not do so, and the mistake not be discovered until after the next succeeding service has been delivered, the mistake shall stand, and a "Let" cannot be claimed or allowed, and the players' positions shall not be corrected.

Singles Play

Rule 13. In singles Rules 9 and 12 hold good, except that—

(a) The players shall serve from and receive service in their respective right-hand service courts only when the server's score is 0 or an even number of points in the game, the service being delivered from and received in their respective left-hand service courts when the server's score is an odd number of points. Setting does not affect this sequence.

(b) Both players shall change service courts after each point has been scored.

Rule 14. Faults. A fault made by a player of the side which is "In" puts the server out; if made by a player whose side is "Out," it counts a point to the "In" side.

It is a fault—

(a) If in serving, (i) the shuttle at the instant of being struck be higher than the server's waist, or (ii) if at the instant of the shuttle being struck the shaft of the racket be not pointing in a downward direction to such an extent that the whole of the head of the racket is discernibly below the whole of the server's hand holding the racket.

(b) If, in serving, the shuttle does not pass over the net, or falls into the wrong service court (*i.e.,* into the one not diagonally opposite to the server), or falls short of the short service line, or beyond the long service line, or outside the side boundary lines of the service court into which service is in order.

(c) If the server's feet are not in the service court from which service is at the time being in order, or if the feet of the player receiving the service are not in the service court diagonally opposite until the service is delivered. (*Vide* Rule 16).

(d) If before or during the delivery of the service any player makes preliminary feints or otherwise intentionally balks his opponent, or if any player deliberately delays serving the shuttle or in getting ready to receive it so as to obtain an unfair advantage.

(e) If in either service or play, the shuttle falls outside the boundaries of the court, or passes through or under the net, or fails to pass the net, or touches the roof or side walls, or the person or dress of a player. (A shuttle falling on a line shall be deemed to have fallen in the court or service court of which such line is a boundary.)

(f) If the shuttle "In Play" be struck before it crosses to the striker's side of the net. (The striker may, however, follow the shuttle over the net with his racket in the course of his stroke.)

(g) If, when the shuttle is "In Play," a player touches the net or its supports with racket, person or dress.

(h) If the shuttle be caught and held on the racket and then slung during the execution of a stroke; or if the shuttle be hit twice in succession by the same player with two strokes; or if the shuttle be hit by a player and his partner successively.

(i) If, in play, a player strikes the shuttle (unless he thereby makes a good return) or is struck by it, whether he is standing within or outside the boundaries of the court.

(j) If a player obstructs an opponent.

(k) If Rule 16 be transgressed.

General

Rule 15. The server may not serve till his opponent is ready, but the opponent shall be deemed to be ready if a return of the service be attempted.

Rule 16. The server and the player served to must stand within the limits of their respective service courts (as bounded by the short and long service, the center, and side lines), and some part of both feet of these players must remain in contact with the surface of the court in a stationary position until the service is delivered. A foot on or touching a line in the case of either the server or the receiver shall be held to be outside his service court. (*Vide* Rule 14(c).) The respective partners may take up any position, provided they do not unsight or otherwise obstruct an opponent.

Rule 17.

(a) If, in the course of service or rally, the shuttle touches and passes over the net, the stroke is not invalidated thereby. It is a good return if the shuttle having passed outside either post drop on or within the boundary lines of the opposite court. A "Let" may be given by the umpire for any unforeseen or accidental hindrance.

(b) If, in service, or during a rally, a shuttle *after passing over the net, is caught in or on the net,* it is a "Let."

(c) If the receiver is faulted for moving before the service is delivered, or for not being within the correct service court, in accordance with

Rules 14(c) or 16, and at the same time the server is also faulted for a service infringement, it shall be a "Let."

(d) When a "Let" occurs, the play since the last service shall not count, and the player who served shall serve again, except when Rule 12 is applicable.

Rule 18. If the server, in attempting to serve, misses the shuttle, it is not a fault; but if the shuttle be touched by the racket, a service is thereby delivered.

Rule 19. If, when in play, the shuttle strikes the net and remains suspended there, or strikes the net and falls toward the surface of the court on the striker's side of the net, or hits the surface outside the court and an opponent then touches the net or shuttle with his racket or person, there is no penalty, as the shuttle is not *then* in play.

Rule 20. If a player has a chance of striking the shuttle in a downward direction when quite near the net, his opponent must not put up his racket near the net on the chance of the shuttle rebounding from it. This is obstruction within the meaning of Rule 14(j).

A player may, however, hold up his racket to protect his face from being hit if he does not thereby balk his opponent.

Reprinted with the permission of the U.S. Badminton Association, Box 237, Swartz Creek, Mich. 48473.

THE RULES OF PLATFORM TENNIS

Rule 5. Doubles Only. Platform tennis customarily is played only as a game of *doubles,* with two players on each side. The side that is serving is called the *serving team,* and the other side is called the *receiving team.*

Although singles may be played for fun or practice, there are no singles tournament competitions.

Rule 6. Choice of Sides and Service. The choice of sides and the right to serve first or to receive first is decided by toss, which is generally accomplished by spinning the paddle.

The team that does not toss has the right to call the toss. The team winning the toss has the following options:

(a) The right to serve first, in which case the other team has the right to choose from which end of the court to receive;

(b) the right to receive first, in which case the other team has the right to choose from which end of the court to serve;

(c) the right to choose the end, in which case the other team has the right to elect to serve first or to receive first;

(d) the right to require the other team to make the first choice.

Rule 7. Server and Receiver. After the toss has been concluded, the teams take their places on opposite sides of the net. The member of the serving team who elects to serve first becomes the *server*. The member of the receiving team who elects to play the right court becomes the first *receiver*.

The server must deliver service from a position behind the baseline and between the center mark and the sideline, diagonally crosscourt from the receiver.

The receiver may stand wherever he pleases on his own side of the net, on or off the court. Likewise the server's partner and the receiver's partner may take any position they choose on their own sides of the net, on or off the court.

The server alternates serving, first from behind his own right court into the receiver's right service court, then from behind his own left court in to the receiver's left service court, and so on. Members of the receiving team alternate receiving service.

If the server serves from behind the wrong court and his mistake is not discovered until the point has been completed, the point stands as played, but thereafter the server must serve from the correct court according to the score. If the server serves from behind the wrong court and the mistake is detected by the receiving team after the service has been delivered and that team does not attempt to return the service, the server loses the point.

The ball served must pass over the net cleanly and hit the deck within the proper service court before the receiver may return it. Receiver may not volley the serve, *i.e.*, strike the ball before it has bounced. If he does so, receiver loses the point outright.

Rule 8. Delivery of the Service. The service is delivered as follows: the server takes an initial position behind the baseline and between an imaginary extension of the center mark and the sideline, as described in Rule 7. The server then projects the ball by hand into the air in any direction, and before it hits the ground strikes the ball with his paddle. At the moment of impact the service delivery is completed.

Rule 9. Only One Service. Only one service is allowed. If the service is a fault, the server loses the point. If the service is a let, the server serves the point again.

Rule 10. Fault or Out. The serve is a fault if:

(a) the server does not take a legal position as described in Rules 7 and 8;

(b) the server commits a footfault (see Rule 11);

(c) the server misses the ball completely in attempting to strike it;

(d) the ball does not land in the proper service court;

(e) the ball served hits the server's partner;

(f) the ball touches a court fixture other than the net, band or center strap before it hits the deck. If it touches any of the above fixtures and then lands within the proper service court, it is a let (see Rule 13);

A *ball in play* (other than a serve) is out if it does not land within the court on the proper side of the net after either crossing the net or touching the net, post, cord, band or center strap.

Rule 11. Footfault. The server shall, throughout delivery of the service, up to the moment of impact of paddle and ball:

(a) Not change his position by walking or running.

(b) Not touch, with either foot, any area other than that behind the baseline within the imaginary extension of the center mark and the sideline.

Rule 12. Receiving Team Must Be Ready. The server must not deliver his serve until the receiving team is ready. If the receiver makes any attempt to return the ball, he is deemed to be ready. Also, if the receiver attempts to return the ball it is deemed that his partner also is ready.

If the receiver says that he is not ready as a serve is being delivered, the serve shall be played again, provided the receiver does not attempt to return the ball. In such case, the receiver may not claim a fault should the serve land outside the service court.

Rule 13. A Let. In all cases where a let is called, the point is to be replayed.

The *service* is a let if:

(a) it touches the net, cord, center strap or band and then lands in the proper service court;

(b) after touching the net, band or center strap it touches either member of the receiving team or anything they are wearing or carrying before hitting the deck, regardless of where they might be standing, on or off the court;

(c) it is delivered when the receiving team is not ready (see Rule 12).

A *ball in play* is a let if:

(d) it hits an overhanging obstruction such as a tree limb or a crossbeam;

(e) the ball becomes broken in the course of a point;

(f) play is interrupted by an accidental occurrence such as a ball from another court bouncing into the court.

Rule 14. Serve Touching Receiving Team. If the serve touches the receiver or the receiver's partner or anything they are wearing or carrying before the ball has hit the deck, the server wins the point outright, provided the serve is not a let as described in Rule 13(b). This ruling applies whether the member of the receiving team is hit while he is standing on or off the court.

Rule 15. When Receiver Becomes Server. At the end of the first game of a set the receiving team becomes the serving team. The partners decide between them who will serve first in each set. The order of service remains in force for that entire set.

Rule 16. Serving or Receiving Out of Turn. If a player serves out of turn, the player who should be serving must take over the serving from the point that the mistake is discovered. All points stand as played.

If an entire game is served by the wrong player, the game score stands as played, but the order of service remains as altered, so that in no case may one player on a team serve three games in a row.

If the receiving team receives from the wrong sides of their court (as established in their first receiving game of the set) they must play that entire game from the "wrong courts" but must revert to the original sides of their court the next game they are receivers.

Rule 17. Ball Remains in Play. Once a ball is put into play by service, it remains in play until the point is decided, unless a fault or a let is called.

Rule 18. Loss of Point. A team loses the point if:

(a) the ball bounces a second time on its side of the net, provided the first bounce was within the court;

(b) a player returns the ball in such a way that it hits:

i. the deck on the other side of the net outside the sidelines or baseline;

ii. any object, other than an opposing player, on the other side of the net outside the sidelines or baseline;

iii. the net, post, cord, band or center strap and does not then land within the court on the other side of the net.

(c) a player volleys the ball and fails to make a good return, even when standing outside the court;

(d) a player touches or strikes the ball more than once in making a stroke (commonly called a double hit or "carry");

(e) a player volleys the ball before it has crossed over to his side of the net, *i.e.*, reaches over the net to strike the ball, making contact on the opponents' side of the net; See Rule 20(b).

(f) a player is touched by a ball in play, unless it is a let service (see Rule 13b);

(g) a player throws his paddle at the ball in play and hits it;

(h) a player bounces the ball over the screen and out of the enclosure or into a lighting fixture, whether or not the ball rebounds back into the court.

(i) a player or anything he wears or carries touches the net, post, cord, band or center strap, or the court surface on the opponents' side of the net, within the boundary lines, while the ball is in play.

Rule 19. Ball Touching Court Fixtures. If the ball in play touches a Court Fixture (as defined in Rule 2) after it has hit the deck within the boundaries of the court, the ball remains in play and may be returned, so long as it has not hit the deck a second time on the same side of the net.

EXCEPTIONS: If the ball hits a lighting fixture, the point is concluded —loss of point for striker. If the ball hits a crossbeam it is a let.

In matches in which an Umpire and an Umpire's chair are inside the enclosure, a ball striking either the Umpire or his chair prior to landing in the opponents' court is loss of point for the striker.

Rule 20. Good Return. It is a good return if:

(a) the ball touches the net, posts, cord, band or center strap and then hits the deck within the proper court;

(b) the ball, served or returned, hits the deck within the proper court and rebounds or is blown back over the net, and the player whose turn it is to strike reaches over the net and plays the ball, provided that neither he nor any part of his clothing or equipment touches the net, posts, cord, band or center strap or the deck within his opponents' court, and that the stroke is otherwise good. (See also Rule 21, Interference.)

(c) the ball is returned outside the post, either above or below the level of the top of the net, whether or not it touches the post, provided that it then hits the deck within the proper court.

NOTE: It is not a good return if the ball is hit through the open space between the net and the post.

(d) a player's paddle passes over the net after he has returned the ball, provided that the ball had crossed to his side of the net before being struck by him, and that the stroke is otherwise good.

Rule 21. Interference. In case a player is hindered in making a stroke by anything not within his control, the point is replayed.

Rule 22. Scoring.

(a) *The Game:*

The first point is called 15, although it is also commonly called 5.
The second point is called 30.
The third point is called 40.
The fourth point is Game.
When both teams score 15, or both score 30, the score is called "15 all" or "30 all."

When both teams score 40, the score is called Deuce.

The next point after Deuce is called Advantage for the team winning it, thus Advantage Server (or more usually Ad In), if the serving team wins, and Advantage Receiver (or Ad Out), if the receiving team wins.

If the team with the Advantage wins the next point, it wins the game. If the other team wins that point, the score reverts to Deuce. This continues indefinitely until one or the other team wins two points in a row from Deuce, which wins the game.

Zero, or no points, is called Love. A game that is won "at love" means that the losing team scored no points.

(b) *The Set:*

The team which first wins 6 games wins the Set. However, the winning team must have a margin of 2 games, and a set played under the traditional rules continues until one team has such a 2 game margin, *e.g.*, 8-6 or 11-9.

A set that is won "at love" means that the losing team scored no games.

Should the players or the tournament committee decide to play a Tiebreak, a special procedure is followed when the game score is 6 all. The APTA recommends the use of the 12 point Tiebreak, especially when time is a problem. Tournament Committees should announce in the tournament rules whether the Tiebreak is to be played.

(c) *The Match:* Customarily a match is best of 3 sets but a Tournament Committee has the right to require best of 5 in the late rounds or the finals of a Men's Tournament.

Reprinted with the permission of the American Platform Tennis Association, 52 Upper Montclair Plaza, Upper Montclair, N.J. 07043.

THE RULES OF RACQUETBALL

Part IV. Play Regulations

Rule 4.1. Serve—Generally.

(a) *Order.* The player or side winning the toss becomes the first server and starts the first game. The loser of the toss will serve first in the second game. The player or team scoring more points in games one and two combined shall serve first in the tie-breaker. In the event that both players or teams score an equal number of points in the first two games, another coin toss shall be held prior to the tie-breaker with the winner of the toss serving first.

(b) *Start.* Games are started from any place within the service zone. No part of either foot may extend beyond either line of the service zone. Stepping on the line (but not beyond it) is permitted. Server must remain in the service zone until the served ball passes the short line. Violations are called "foot faults."

(c) *Manner.* A serve is commenced by bouncing the ball to the floor in the service zone, and on the first bounce the ball is struck by the server's racquet so that it hits the front wall and on the rebound hits the floor back of the short line, either with or without touching one of the side walls.

(d) *Readiness.* Serves shall not be made until the receiving side is ready, or the referee has called play ball.

(e) *Deliberate Delays.* Deliberate delays on the part of the server or receiver exceeding 10 seconds shall result in an out or point against the offender.

(1) This "10 second rule" is applicable to both server and receiver, each of whom is allowed up to 10 seconds to serve or be ready to receive. It is the server's responsibility to look and to be certain the receiver is ready. If the receiver is not ready, he must signal so by raising his racquet above his head. Such raising of the racquet is the only legal signal that the receiver may make to alert the referee and server that he is not ready.

(2) If the server serves a ball while the receiver is signaling "not ready" the serve shall go over with no penalty.

(3) If the server looks at the receiver and the receiver is not signaling "not ready" the server may then serve. If the receiver attempts to signal "not ready" after this point, such signal shall not be acknowledged and the serve becomes legal.

(f) *Time-Outs.* At no time shall a call of "time-out" by a player be acknowledged by the referee if the "time-out" call does not precede the serve, *i.e.,* the so-called Chabot time-out is not legal. The beginning of the serve, as indicated in Rule 4.1c, is with the bounce of the ball.

Rule 4.2. Serve—In Doubles.

(a) *Server.* At the beginning of each game in doubles, each side shall inform the referee of the order of service, which order shall be followed throughout the game. Only the first server serves the first time up and continues to serve first throughout the game. When the first server is out —the side is out. Thereafter both players on each side shall serve until a handout occurs. It is not necessary for the server to alternate serves to their opponents.

(b) *Partner's Position.* On each serve, the server's partner shall stand erect with his back to the side wall and with both feet on the floor within the service box until the served ball passes the short line. Violations are called "foot faults," subject to penalties thereof.

Rule 4.3. Defective Serves. Defective serves are of three types resulting in penalties as follows:

(a) *Dead Ball Serve.* A dead ball serve results in no penalty and the server is given another serve without canceling a prior illegal serve.

(b) *Fault Serve.* Two fault serves result in a handout.

(c) *Out Serves.* An out serve results in a handout.

Rule 4.4. Dead Ball Serves. Dead ball serves do not cancel any previous illegal serve. They occur when an otherwise legal serve:

(a) *Hits Partner.* Hits the server's partner on the fly on the rebound from the front wall while the server's partner is in the service box. Any serve that touches the floor before hitting the partner in the box is a short.

(b) *Screen Balls.* Passes too close to the server or the server's partner to obstruct the view of the returning side. Any serve passing behind the server's partner and the side wall is an automatic screen.

(c) *Court Hinders.* Hits any part of the court that under local rules is a dead ball.

Rule 4.5. Fault Serves. The following serves are faults and any two in succession results in a handout:

(a) *Foot Faults.* A foot fault results:

(1) When the server leaves the service zone before the served ball passes the short line.

(2) When the server's partner leaves the service box before the served ball passes the short line.

(b) *Short Service.* A short service is any served ball that first hits the front wall and on the rebound hits the floor in front of the back edge of the short line either with or without touching one side wall.

(c) *Three-Wall Serve.* A three-wall serve is any ball served that first hits the front wall and on the rebound hits two side walls on the fly.

(d) *Ceiling Serve.* A ceiling serve is any served ball that touches the ceiling after hitting the front wall either with or without touching one side wall.

(e) *Long Serve.* A long serve is any served ball that first hits the front wall and rebounds to the back wall before touching the floor.

(f) *Out of Court Serve*. Any ball going out of the court on the serve.

Rule 4.6. Out Serves. Any one of the following serves results in a hand-out:

(a) A serve in which the ball is struck after being bounced outside the service zone.

(b) *Missed Ball*. Any attempt to strike the ball on the first bounce that results either in a total miss or in touching any part of the server's body other than his racquet.

(c) *Non-front Serve*. Any served ball that strikes the server's partner, or the ceiling, floor or side wall, before striking the front wall.

(d) *Touched Serve*. Any served ball that on the rebound from the front wall touches the server or touches the server's partner while any part of his body is out of the service box or the server's partner intentionally catches the served ball on the fly.

(e) *Out-of-Order Serve*. In doubles, when either partner serves out of order.

(f) *Crotch Serve*. If the served ball hits the crotch in the front wall it is considered the same as hitting the floor and is an out. A crotch serve into the back wall (or side wall on three-wall serves) is good and in play.

Rule 4.7. Return of Serve.

(a) The receiver or receivers may not infringe on the "five foot zone" until the server strikes the ball. The receiver may then "rush" the serve and return it after the served ball passes the short line, as long as no part of the receiver's body or racquet breaks the plane of the service zone.

(b) *Defective Serve*. To eliminate any misunderstanding, the receiving side should not catch or touch a defectively served ball until called by the referee or it has touched the floor the second time.

(c) *Fly Return*. In making a fly return the receiver must end up with both feet back of the service zone. A violation by a receiver results in a point for the server.

(d) *Legal Return*. After the ball is legally served, one of the players on the receiving side must strike the ball with his racquet either on the fly or after the first bounce and before the ball touches the floor the second time to return the ball to the front wall either directly or after touching one or both side walls, the back wall or the ceiling, or any combination of those surfaces. A returned ball may not touch the floor before touching the front wall. (1) It is legal to return the ball by striking the ball into the back wall first, then hitting the front wall on the fly or after hitting the side wall or ceiling. (2) If the ball should strike the front wall, then back wall and then front wall again without striking the floor, the player whose turn it is to strike the ball may do so by letting the ball bounce after hitting the front wall a second time. (3) If the ball strikes the front wall, then back wall, and then front wall again after striking the floor, the player whose turn it is to strike the ball must do so by striking it before it hits the floor a second time.

(e) *Failure to Return.* The failure to return a serve results in a point for the server.

Rule 4.8. Changes of Serve

(a) *Handout.* A server is entitled to continue serving until:

(1) *Out Serve.* He makes an out serve under Rule 4.6 or

(2) *Fault Serves.* He makes two fault serves in succession under Rule 4.5, or

(3) *Hits Partner.* He hits his partner with an attempted return, or

(4) *Return Failure.* He or his partner fails to keep the ball in play by returning it as required by Rule 4.7(d), or

(5) *Avoidable Hinder.* He or his partner commits an avoidable hinder under Rule 4.11.

(b) *Side-out.*

(1) In Singles. In singles, retiring the server retires the side.

(2) In Doubles. In doubles, the side is retired when both partners have been put out, except on the first serve as provided in Rule 4.2 (a).

(c) *Effect.* When the server or the side loses the serve, the server or serving side shall become the receiver; and the receiver or receiving side, the server; and so alternately in all subsequent services of the game.

Rule 4.9. Rallies. Each legal return after the serve is called a rally. Play during rallies shall be according to the following rules:

(a) *One or Both Hands.* Only the head of the racquet may be used at any time to return the ball. The ball must be hit with the racquet in one or both hands. Switching hands to hit a ball is an out. The use of any portion of the body is an out.

(b) *One Touch.* In attempting returns, the ball may be touched only once by one player on returning side. In doubles both partners may swing at, but only one may hit, the ball. Each violation of (a) or (b) results in a handout or point.

(c) *Return Attempts.*

(1) *In Singles.* In singles if a player swings at but misses the ball in play, the player may repeat his attempts to return the ball until it touches the floor the second time.

(2) *In Doubles*. In doubles if one player swings at but misses the ball, both he and his partner may make further attempts to return the ball until it touches the floor the second time. Both partners on a side are entitled to an attempt to return the ball.

(3) *Hinders*. In singles or doubles, if a player swings at but misses the ball in play and in his or his partner's attempt again to play the ball there is an unintentional interference by an opponent it shall be a hinder. (See Rule 4.10).

(d) *Touching Ball*. Except as provided in Rule 4.10(a) (2), any touching of a ball before it touches the floor the second time by a player other than the one making a return is a point or out against the offending player.

(e) *Out of Court Ball*.

(1) *After Return*. Any ball returned to the front wall which on the rebound or on the first bounce goes into the gallery or through any opening in a side wall shall be declared dead and the serve replayed.

(2) *No Return*. Any ball not returned to the front wall, but which caroms off a player's racquet into the gallery or into any opening in a side wall either with or without touching the ceiling, side or back wall, shall be an out or point against the player or players failing to make the return.

(f) *Dry Ball*. During the game and particularly on service every effort should be made to keep the ball dry. Deliberate wetting shall result in an out.

(g) *Broken Ball*. If there is any suspicion that the ball has broken during the serve, or during a rally, play shall continue until the end of the rally. The referee or any player may request the ball be examined. If the referee decides the ball is broken or otherwise defective, a new ball shall be put into play and the rally replayed.

(h) *Ball Inspection*. The ball may be inspected by the referee between rallies at any time during a match.

(i) *Play Stoppage*.

(1) If a player loses a shoe or other equipment, or foreign objects enter the court, or any other outside interference occurs, the referee shall stop the play.

(2) Players wearing protective eyeglasses have the responsibility of having such eyeglasses securely fastened. In the event that such protective eyeglasses should become unfastened and enter the court, the play shall be stopped as long as such eyeglasses were fastened initially. In the event such eyeglasses are not securely fastened, no stoppage of

play shall result and the player wearing such glasses plays at his own risk.

(3) If a player loses control of his racquet, time should be called after the point has been decided, providing the racquet does not strike an opponent or interfere with ensuing play.

Rule 4.10. Dead Ball Hinders. Hinders are of two types—"dead ball" and "avoidable." Dead ball hinders as described in this rule result in the rally being replayed. Avoidable hinders are described in Rule 4.11.

(a) *Situations*. When called by the referee, the following are dead ball hinders:

(1) *Court Hinders*. Hits any part of the court which under local rules is a dead ball.

(2) *Hitting Opponent*. Any returned ball that touches an opponent on the fly before it returns to the front wall.

(3) *Body Contact*. Any body contact with an opponent that interferes with seeing or returning the ball.

(4) *Screen Ball*. Any ball rebounding from the front wall close to the body of a player on the side which just returned the ball to interfere with or prevent the returning side from seeing the ball. See Rule 4.4 (b).

(5) *Straddle Ball*. A ball passing between the legs of a player on the side which just returned the ball, if there is no fair chance to see or return the ball.

(6) *Back Swing Hinder*. If there is body contact on the backswing, the player must call it immediately. This is the only hinder call a player can make.

(7) *Other Interference*. Any other unintentional interference which prevents an opponent from having a fair chance to see or return the ball.

(b) *Effect*. A call by the referee of a "hinder" stops the play and voids any situation following, such as the ball hitting a player. No player is authorized to call a hinder, except on the backswing and such a call must be made immediately, as provided in Rule 4.10(a)(6).

(c) *Avoidance*. While making an attempt to return the ball, a player is entitled to a fair chance to see and return the ball. It is the duty of the side that has just served or returned the ball to move so that the receiving side may go straight to the ball and not be required to go around an opponent. The referee should be liberal in calling hinders to discourage any practice of playing the ball where an adversary cannot see it until too late. It is no excuse that the ball is "killed," unless in the opinion of the referee the ball couldn't be returned. Hinders should be called without a claim by a player, especially in close plays and on game points.

(d) *In Doubles*. In doubles, both players on a side are entitled to a fair and unobstructed chance at the ball and either one is entitled to a hinder even though naturally it would be his partner's ball and even though his partner may have attempted to play the ball or that he may already have missed it. It is not a hinder when one player hinders his partner.

Rule 4.11. Avoidable Hinders. An avoidable hinder results in an "out" or a point depending upon whether the offender was serving or receiving.

(a) *Failure to Move*. Does not move sufficiently to allow opponent his shot.

(b) *Blocking*. Moves into a position effecting a block, on the opponent about to return the ball, or, in doubles, one partner moves in front of an opponent as his partner is returning the ball.

(c) *Moving into Ball*. Moves in the way and is struck by the ball just played by his opponent.

(d) *Pushing*. Deliberately pushing or shoving an opponent during a rally.

Reprinted with the permission of the U.S. Racquetball Association, 4101 Dempster Street, Skokie, Ill. 60076.

THE RULES OF SQUASH

Singles

Rule 1. Server. At the start of a match the choice to serve or receive shall be decided by the spin of a racquet. The server retains the serve until he loses a point, in which event he loses the serve.

Rule 2. Service.

(a) The server, until the ball has left the racquet from the service, must stand with at least one foot on the floor within and not touching the line surrounding the service box and serve the ball onto the front wall above the service line and below the 16′ line before it touches any other part of the court, so that on its rebound (return) it first strikes the floor within, but not touching, the lines of the opposite service court, either before or after touching any other wall or walls within the court. A ball so served is a good service, otherwise it is a Fault.

(b) If the first service is a Fault, the server shall serve again from the same side. If the server makes two consecutive Faults, he loses the point. A service called a Fault may not be played, but the receiver may volley any service which has struck the front wall in accordance with this rule.

(c) At the beginning of each game, and each time there is a new server, the ball shall be served by the winner of the previous point from whichever service box the server elects and thereafter alternately until the service is lost or until the end of the game. If the server serves from the wrong box there shall be no penalty and the service shall count as if served from the correct box, provided, however, that if the receiver does not attempt to return the service, he may demand that it be served from the other box, or if, before the receiver attempts to return the service, the Referee calls a Let (See Rule 9), the service shall be made from the other box.

(d) A ball is in play from the moment at which it is delivered in service until (1) the point is decided; (2) a Fault, as defined in 2(a) is made; or (3) a Let or Let Point occurs. (See Rules 9 and 10.)

Rule 3. Return of Service and Subsequent Play.

(a) A return is deemed to be made at the instant the ball touches the racquet of the player making the return. To make a good return of a service or of a subsequent return the ball must be struck on the volley or before it has touched the floor twice, and reach the front wall on the fly above the tell-tale and below the 16' line, and it may touch any wall or walls within the court before or after reaching the front wall. On any return the ball may be struck only once. It may not be "carried" or "double-hit."

(b) If the receiver fails to make a good return of a good service, the server wins the point. If the receiver makes a good return of service, the players shall alternate making returns until one player fails to make a good return. The player failing to make a good return loses the point.

(c) Until the ball has been touched or has hit the floor twice, it may be struck at any number of times.

(d) If at any time after a service the ball hits outside the playing surfaces of the court (the ceiling and/or lights, or on or above a line marking the perimeters of the playing surfaces of the court), the player so hitting the ball loses the point, unless a Let or a Let Point occurs (See Rules 9 and 10.)

Rule 4. Score. Each point won by a player shall add one to his score.

Rule 5. Game. The player who first scores fifteen points wins the game excepting that:

(a) At "thirteen all" the player who has first reached the score of thirteen must elect one of the following before the next serve:

(1) Set to five points—making the game eighteen points.

(2) Set to three points—making the game sixteen points.

(3) No set, in which event the game remains fifteen points.

(b) At "fourteen all" provided the score has not been "thirteen all" the player who has first reached the score of fourteen must elect one of the following before the next serve:

(1) Set to three points—making the game seventeen points.

(2) No set, in which event the game remains fifteen points.

Rule 6. Match. The player who first wins three games wins the match, except that a player may be awarded the match at any time upon the retirement, default or disqualification of an opponent.

Rule 7. Right to Play Ball. Immediately after striking the ball a player must get out of an opponent's way and must:

(a) Give an opponent a fair view of the ball, provided, however, interference purely with an opponent's vision in following the flight of the ball is not a Let (see Rule 9).

(b) Give an opponent a fair opportunity to get to and/or strike at the ball in and from any position on the court elected by the opponent; and

(c) Allow an opponent to play the ball to any part of the front wall or to either side wall near the front wall.

Rule 8. Ball in Play Touching Player.

(a) If a ball in play, after hitting the front wall, but before being returned again, shall touch either player, or anything he wears or carries (other than the racquet of the player who makes the return), the player so touched loses the point, except as provided in Rule 9(a) or 9(b).

(b) If a ball in play touches the player who last returned it or anything he wears or carries before it hits the front wall, the player so touched loses the point.

(c) If a ball in play, after being struck by a player on a return, hits the player's opponent or anything the opponent wears or carries before reaching the front wall:

(1) The player who made the return shall lose the point if the return would not have been good.

(2) The player who made the return shall win the point if the ball, except for such interference, would have hit the front wall fairly; provided, however, the point shall be a Let (see Rule 9) if:

(i) The ball would have touched some other wall before so hitting the front wall.

(ii) The ball has hit some other wall before hitting the player's opponent or anything he wears or carries.

(iii) The player who made the return shall have turned following the ball around prior to playing the ball.

(d) If a player strikes at and misses the ball, he may make further attempts to return it. If, after being missed, the ball touches his opponent or anything he wears or carries:

(1) If the player might otherwise have made a good return, the point shall be a Let.

(2) If the player could not have made a good return, he shall lose the point.

If any further attempt is successful but the ball, before reaching the front wall, touches his opponent or anything he wears or carries and Rule 8(c)(2) applies, the point shall be a Let.

(e) When there is no referee, if the player who made the return does not concede that the return would not have been good, or, alternatively, the player's opponent does not concede that the ball has hit him (or anything he wears or carries) and would have gone directly to the front wall without first touching any other wall, the point shall be a Let.

(f) When there is no referee, if the players are unable to agree whether 8(d)(1) or 8(d)(2) applies, the point shall be a Let.

Rule 9. Let. A Let is the playing over of a point.

On the replay of the point the server (1) is entitled to two serves even if a Fault was called on the original point, (2) must serve from the correct box even if he served from the wrong box on the original point, and (3) provided he is a new server, may serve from a service box other than the one selected on the original point.

In addition to the Lets described in Rules 2(c) and 8(c)(2), the following are Lets if the player whose turn it is to strike the ball could otherwise have made a good return:

(a) When such player's opponent violates Rule 7.

(b) When owing to the position of such player, his opponent is unable to avoid being touched by the ball.

(c) When such player refrains from striking at the ball because of a reasonable fear of injuring his opponent.

(d) When such player before or during the act of striking or striking at the ball is touched by his opponent, his racquet or anything he wears or carries.

(e) When on the first bounce from the floor the ball hits on or above the six and one half foot line on the back wall; and

(f) When a ball in play breaks. If a player thinks the ball has broken while play is in progress he must nevertheless complete the point and then immediately request a Let, giving the ball to the Referee for inspection. The Referee shall allow a Let only upon such immediate request if the ball in fact proves to be broken (See Rule 13(c).

A player may request a Let or a Let Point (See Rule 10). A request by a player for a Let shall automatically include a request for a Let Point. Upon such request, the Referee shall allow a Let, Let Point or no Let.

No Let shall be allowed on any stroke a player makes unless he requests such before or during the act of striking or striking at the ball.

The Referee may not call or allow a Let as defined in this Rule 9 unless such Let is requested by a player; provided, however, the Referee may call a Let at any time (1) when there is interference with play caused by any factor beyond the control of the players, or (2) when he fears that a player is about to suffer severe physical injury.

Rule 10. Let Point. A Let Point is the awarding of a point to a player when an opponent unnecessarily violates Rule (7(b) or 7(c).

An unnecessary violation occurs (1) when the player fails to make the necessary effort within the scope of his normal ability to avoid the violation, thereby depriving his opponent of a clear opportunity to attempt a winning shot, or (2) when the player has repeatedly failed to make the necessary effort within the scope of his normal ability to avoid such violations.

The Referee may not award a Let Point as defined in this Rule 10 unless such Let Point or a Let (see Rule 9) is requested by a player.

When there is no referee, if a player does not concede that he has unnecessarily violated Rule 7(b) or 7(c), the point shall be a Let.

Reprinted with the permission of the U.S. Squash Racquets Association, 211 Ford Road, Bala Cynwyd, Pa. 19004.

THE RULES OF TENNIS

The Singles Game

Rule 4. Server and Receiver. The Players shall stand on opposite sides of the net; the player who first delivers the ball shall be called the Server, and the other the Receiver.

Rule 5. Choice of Ends and Service. The choice of ends and the right to be Server or Receiver in the first game shall be decided by toss. The player winning the toss may choose, or require his opponent to choose:

(a) The right to be Server or Receiver, in which case the other player shall choose the end; or

(b) The end, in which case the other player shall choose the right to be Server or Receiver.

Rule 6. Delivery of Service. The service shall be delivered in the following manner. Immediately before commencing to serve, the Server shall stand with both feet at rest behind (*i.e.,* farther from the net than) the base-line, and within the imaginary continuations of the center-mark and side-line. The Server shall then project the ball by hand into the air in any direction and before it hits the ground strike it with his racket, and the delivery shall be deemed to have been completed at the moment of the impact of the racket and the ball. A player with the use of only one arm may utilize his racket for the projection.

Rule 7. Foot Fault. The Server shall throughout the delivery of the service:

(a) Not change his position by walking or running.

(b) Not touch, with either foot, any area other than that behind the base-line within the imaginary extension of the center-mark and sideline.

Rule 8. From Alternate Courts.

(a) In delivering the service, the Server shall stand alternately behind the right and left Courts, beginning from the right in every game. If service from a wrong half of the Court occurs and is undetected, all play resulting from such wrong service or services shall stand, but the inaccuracy of the station shall be corrected immediately it is discovered.

(b) The ball served shall pass over the net and hit the ground within the Service Court which is diagonally opposite, or upon any line bounding such Court before the Receiver returns it.

Rule 9. Faults. The Service is a fault:

(a) If the Server commit any breach of Rules 6, 7 or 8;

(b) If he miss the ball in attempting to strike it;

(c) If the ball served touch a permanent fixture (other than the net, strap or band) before it hits the ground.

Rule 10. Service After a Fault. After a fault (if it be the first fault) the Server shall serve again from behind the same half of the Court from which he served that fault, unless the service was from the wrong half, when in accordance with Rule 8, the Server shall be entitled to one service only from behind the other half. A fault may not be claimed after the next service has been delivered.

Rule 11. Receiver Must Be Ready. The Server shall not serve until the Receiver is ready. If the latter attempts to return the service, he shall be deemed ready. If, however, the Receiver signify that he is not ready, he may not claim a fault because the ball does not hit the ground within the limits fixed for the service.

Rule 12. A Let. In all cases where a let has to be called under the rules, or to provide for an interruption to play, it shall have the following interpretations:

(a) When called solely in respect of a service, that one service only shall be replayed.

(b) When called under any other circumstance, the point shall be replayed.

Rule 13. The Service Is a Let. The service is a let:

(a) If the ball served touch the net, strap or band, and is otherwise good, or, after touching the net, strap or band, touch the Receiver or anything which he wears or carries before hitting the ground.

(b) If a service or a fault be delivered when the Receiver is not ready (see Rule 11).

Rule 14. When Receiver Becomes Server. At the end of the first game the Receiver shall become the Server, and the Server Receiver; and so on alternately in all the subsequent games of a match. If a player serve out of turn, the player who ought to have served shall serve as soon as the mistake is discovered, but all points scored before such discovery shall be reckoned. If a game shall have been completed before such discovery, the order of service remains as altered. A fault served before such discovery shall not be reckoned.

Rule 15. Ball in Play Till Point Decided. A ball is in play from the moment at which it is delivered in service. Unless a fault or a let be called, it remains in play until the point is decided.

Rule 16. Server Wins Point. The Server wins the point:

(a) If the ball served, not being a let under Rule 13, touch the Receiver or anything which he wears or carries, before it hits the ground;

(b) If the Receiver otherwise loses the point as provided by Rule 18.

Rule 17. Receiver Wins Point. The Receiver wins the point:

(a) If the Server serve two consecutive faults;

(b) If the Server otherwise lose the point as provided by Rule 18.

Rule 18. Player Loses Point. A player loses the point if:

(a) He fail, before the ball in play has hit the ground twice consecutively, to return it directly over the net (except as provided in Rule 22(a) or (c); or

(b) He return the ball in play so that it hits ground, a permanent fixture, or other object, outside any of the lines which bound his opponent's Court (except as provided in Rule 22(a) and (c); or

(c) He volley the ball and fail to make a good return even when standing outside the Court; or

(d) He touch or strike the ball in play with his racket more than once in making a stroke; or

(e) He or his racket (in his hand or otherwise) or anything which he wears or carries touch the net, posts, cord or metal cable, strap or band, or the ground within his opponent's Court at any time while the ball is in play; or

(f) He volley the ball before it has passed the net; or

(g) The ball in play touching him or anything that he wears or carries, except his racket in his hand or hands or

(h) He throws his racket at and hits the ball.

Rule 19. Player Hinders Opponent. If a player commits any act either deliberate or involuntary which, in the opinion of the Umpire, hinders his opponent in making a stroke, the Umpire shall in the first case award the point to the opponent, and in the second case order the point to be replayed.

Rule 20. Ball Falling on Line—Good. A ball falling on line is regarded as falling in the Court bounded by that line.

Rule 21. Ball Touching Permanent Fixture. If the ball in play touch a permanent fixture (other than the net, posts, cord or metal cable, strap or band) after it has hit the ground, the player who struck it wins the point; if before it hits the ground his opponent wins the point.

Rule 22. Good Return. It is a good return:

(a) If the ball touch the net, posts, cord or metal cable, strap or band, provided that it passes over any of them and hits the ground within the Court; or

(b) If the ball, served or returned, hit the ground within the proper Court and rebound or be blown back over the net, and the player whose turn it is to strike reach over the net and play the ball, provided that neither he nor any part of his clothes or racket touch the net, cords or metal cable, strap or band or the ground within his opponent's Court, and that the stroke be otherwise good; or

(c) If the ball be returned outside the post, either above or below the level of the top of the net, even though it touch the post, provided that it hits the ground within the proper Court; or

(d) If a player's racket pass over the net after he has returned the ball, provided the ball pass the net before being played and be properly returned; or

(e) If a player succeeded in returning the ball, served or in play, which strikes a ball lying in the Court.

Rule 23. Interference. In case a player is hindered in making a stroke by anything not within his control except a permanent fixture to the Court, or except as provided for in Rule 19, the point shall re replayed.

Rule 24. The Game. If a player wins his first point, the score is called *15* for that player; on winning his second point, the score is called *30* for that player; on winning his third point, the score is called *40* for that player, and the fourth point won by a player is scored *game* for that player except as below:

If both players have won three points, the score is called *deuce;* and the next point won by a player is called *advantage* for that player. If the same player wins the next point, he wins the game; if the other player wins the next point, the score is again called *deuce;* and so on until a player wins the two points immediately following the score at deuce, when the game is scored for that player.

Rule 25. The Set. A player (or players) who first wins six games wins a set, except that he must win by a margin of two games over his opponent and where necessary a set shall be extended until this margin be achieved.

Rule 26. When Players Change Ends. The players shall change ends at the end of the first, third and every subsequent alternative game of each set, and at the end of each set unless the total number of games in such set be even, in which case the change is not made until the end of the first game of the next set.

Rule 27. Maximum Number of Sets. The maximum number of sets in a match shall be 5, or where women take part, 3.

The Doubles Game

Rule 33. Order of Service. The order of serving shall be decided at the beginning of each set as follows:

The pair who have to serve in the first game of each set shall decide which partner shall do so and the opposing pair shall decide similarly for the second game. The partner of the player who served in the first game shall serve in the third; the partner of the player who served in the second game shall serve in the fourth, and so on in the same order in all the subsequent games of a set.

Rule 34. Order of Receiving. The order of receiving the service shall be decided at the beginning of each set as follows:

The pair who have to receive the service in the first game shall decide which partner shall receive the first service, and that partner shall continue to receive the first service in every odd game throughout that set. The opposing pair shall likewise decide which partner shall receive the first service in the second game and that partner shall continue to receive the first service in every even game throughout that set. Partners shall receive the service alternately throughout each game.

Rule 35. Service Out of Turn. If a partner serve out of his turn, the partner who ought to have served shall serve as soon as the mistake is discovered, but all points scored, and any faults served, before such discovery shall be reckoned. If a game shall have been completed before such discovery the order of service remains as altered.

Rule 36. Error in Order of Receiving. If during a game the order of receiving the service is changed by the receivers it shall remain as altered until the end of the game in which the mistake is discovered, but the partners shall resume their original order of receiving in the next game of that set in which they are receivers of the service.

Rule 37. Ball Touching Server's Partner Is Fault. The service is a fault as provided for by Rule 9, or if the ball served touch the Server's partner or anything he wears or carries; but if the ball served touch the partner of the Receiver or anything which he wears or carries, not being a let under Rule 13(a), before it hits the ground, the Server wins the point.

Rule 38. Ball Struck Alternately. The ball shall be struck alternately by one or other player of the opposing pairs, and if a player touches the ball in play with his racket in contravention of this Rule, his opponent wins the point.

The 7-of-12 Tiebreaker

The 7-of-12 points tiebreaker is the only one allowed in tournaments requiring International Tennis Federation sanction. The winner of the tiebreaker is the player or team to first reach 7 points with a margin of 2. If the points reach 6-all, play continues until one player or team has a two-point margin. This tiebreaker is often called "lingering death" as opposed to the 5-of-9 or "sudden death" tiebreaker which is won by the first player or team to reach 5 points.

Here is the procedure for the 7-of-12 tiebreaker:

Singles: A serves first point from Right court); B serves points 2 and 3 (Left and Right); A serves points 4 and 5 (Left and Right); B serves point 6 (Left) and after they change ends, point 7 (Right); A serves points 8 and 9 (Left and Right); B serves points 10 and 11 (Left and Right); and A serves point 12 (Left). If points reach 6-all, players change ends and continue as before. A serves point 13 (Right); B serves points 14 and 15 (Left and Right); etc., etc., etc., until one player establishes a margin of two points. Players change ends for one game to start the next set, with Player B to serve first.

Doubles follows the same pattern, with partners preserving the sequence of their serving turns. (Assuming A & B vs. C & D) Player A serves first point (Right); C serves points 2 and 3 (Left and Right); B serves points 4 and 5 (Left and Right); D serves point 6 (Left) and after teams change ends, point 7 (Right) . . . A serves points 8 and 9 (Left and Right); C serves points 10 and 11 (Left and Right), and B serves point 12 (Left) . . . If points reach 6-all, teams change ends and continue as before—B serves point 13 (Right); D serves points 14 and 15 (Left and Right); etc., etc., until one team establishes a margin of two points. Teams change ends for one game to start the next set with team C & D to serve first.

The 5-of-9 Tiebreaker

Singles: If it is Player A's turn to serve the 13th game (at 6-all) he shall serve Points 1 and 2, right court and left court; Player B then serves Points 3 and 4 (Right and Left). Players then change ends, and A serves Points 5 and 6; B serves Points 7 and 8. If the score reaches 4 points all, Player B serves Point 9 from the right or left court at the election of the receiver.

The set shall be recorded as 7 games to 6. The tiebreak counts as one game in reckoning ball-changes.

Player B shall serve first in the set following the playing of the tiebreak (thus assuring that he will be first server if this set also goes into a tiebreak). The players shall "stay for one" after a tiebreak.

Doubles: In doubles the same format as in singles applies, provided that each player shall serve from the same end of the court in the tiebreak game that he has served from during that particular set. (Note that this operates to alter the *sequence* of serving by the partners on the *second-*serving team.)

No-Ad Scoring

The "No-Ad" procedure is simply and precisely what the name implies:

A player need win only four points to win a game. That is, if the score goes to three-points-all (or deuce) the next point decides the game—its game point for both players. The receiver has the right to choose to which court the service is to be delivered on the seventh point.

If a No-Ad set reaches 6 games all, a tiebreaker shall be used which normally would be the 5-of-9.

NOTE: The score-calling may be either in the conventional terms or in simple numbers, *i.e.*, "zero, one, two, three, game."

Reprinted with the permission of the U.S. Tennis Association, 51 East 42nd St., New York, N.Y. 10017.

About the Authors

HERB FITZGIBBON is an avid racquet sports player who has won several U.S. national titles in tennis and platform tennis. He has been a member of the U.S. Davis Cup team and is the holder of an Olympic gold medal for tennis. Formerly squash coach at West Point, FitzGibbon is now involved in a variety of racquet sports activities in New York City.

JEFF BAIRSTOW is the managing editor of *Tennis* magazine. He has coauthored a number of sports books and is an enthusiastic amateur racquet sports player.